New Buckenham

New Buckenham

a planned town at work 1530–1780

Paul Rutledge

Copyright © Paul Rutledge

First published in 2000 by Norfolk Archaeological and Historical Research Group, reprinted 2003.

This edition 2019 published by Poppyland Publishing, Lowestoft, NR32 3BB.
www.poppyland.co.uk
ISBN 978 1 909796 44 7

All rights reserved. No part of this publication may be reproduced, stored in a retrieval system or transmitted by any means, mechanical, photocopying, recording or otherwise, without the written permission of the publishers. Designed and typeset in 11 on 13.2 pt Times New Roman.

Printed by Ashford Colour Press.

Front Cover
Aerial photograph of New Buckenham, 2012, courtesy of Mike Page Photography.

Contents

Acknowledgements	vii
Background and Sources	9
The Market	16
The Cloth Trade	26
Leather	35
Bread, Ale and Beer	40
Milling	50
Butchers and Graziers	51
Fishmongers	55
Dairying	55
Grocers and Medicine	55
Metal and Wood Workers	59
Farmers and Gentlemen	63
Services and Miscellaneous	71
The Poor	73
Comment	74
Tables	77
Appendix I: The Probate Inventory of Robert Turner 1592	84
Appendix II: Glossary to Robert Turner's Inventory	91
Wills and Administrations referred to in the text	94
Principal Sources	98
Bibliography	99
Index	102

Illustrations and Tables

1693 map showing Buckenham Castle, its former deer park and the borough of New Buckenham.   viii

Fig. 1. New Buckenham regional setting and trade links.   11

Fig. 2. New Buckenham and surroundings.   13

Fig. 3. New Buckenham town.   17

Fig. 4. Reconstructions.   18

Fig. 5.1-5.11. Location of trades.   20

Plate 1. A drawing of glass from a window in the George Inn (R74).   40

Plate 2. Trade token issued by Francis Watts in 1657.   40

Plate 3. The market cross reconstructed after 1716.   43

Plate 4. R69, the late-medieval gatehouse of the Verdon family mansion.   43

Plate 5. R12, a house built c.1606 on consolidated marsh.   43

Plate 6. R49, an early 16th century Wealden type house.   44

Plate 7. R80 and R81, late 15th century houses.   44

Plate 8. R19 and R20, 16th and 17th century houses in King Street.   44

Table A: Occupations in New Buckenham 1500-1699.   77

Table B: Traders coming to New Buckenham 1563-1642.   78

Table C: High bailiffs' occupations 1554-5 to 1689-90.   78

Table D: Occupations of charity trustees 1614-1759.   79

Table E: Assessments for stock-in-trade 1704-5 to 1715-16.   80

Table F: Summary of stock-in-trade list 1704-5 to 1715-16.   81

Table G: Stock-in-trade 1750.   82

Table H: Trades in population listing 1803.   82

Acknowledgements

To the first edition (2000)

The potentialities of New Buckenham were first revealed to me by Anthony Rossi's diploma thesis, *New Buckenham, Norfolk, a Study of Conservation in Rural Areas* (York, 1973), and by Dr R.A. Hamerton's giving me access to the borough archives. These he then public-spiritedly placed in the Norfolk Record Office, as did Messrs Pomeroy and Son, through Leonard Breeze, the New Buckenham solicitors' records in their care. My grateful thanks go also to Joan Whitwham for making the New Buckenham parish papers available, to Angela Dain for passing on various references to the *Norwich Gazette*, some of which appear in her MA dissertation, *Assembly Rooms and Houses in Norfolk and Suffolk* (UEA, 1993), to Paul Cattermole, Susan Maddock, Frank Devany, Alison Laurie and Nesta Evans for alerting me to other material, to Alayne Fenner especially for help with Robert Turner's probate inventory, to the County Archivist Dr John Alban for permission to print it, to Chris Barringer and Tony Bradstreet for helpful comments, to John Ayton for maps and other illustrations and editorial oversight, to many individuals who have given me access to title deeds and documents in their possession and, as always, to the staffs of the Norfolk Record Office and the Norfolk Studies Library.

Paul Rutledge

To the second edition (2019)

Thanks are due to the Norfolk Token Project for permission to use the illustration of the token of Francis Watts (Plate 2). They are also due to the present County Archivist, Gary Tuson, for permission to republish the probate inventory of Robert Turner (DN/INV/10/414) and to use the illustrations of the window glass at the George Inn (Rye 17/1) and the map of 1693 (ACC Steel and Co 23/09/1986), to the staff of the Norfolk Record Office, and to John Ayton for agreeing to the reuse and/or reworking of some of his original illustrations. The plans showing the detailed layout of the town (Figs 3 and 4) are based on a map drawn by Phillip Judge. I am grateful to Elizabeth Griffiths for taking photographs of the illustration of the window glass (Plate 1) and of the house featured in Plate 7, and to Peter Stibbons for the other photographs used in Plates 3-8 and for his general help and assistance.

Elizabeth Rutledge

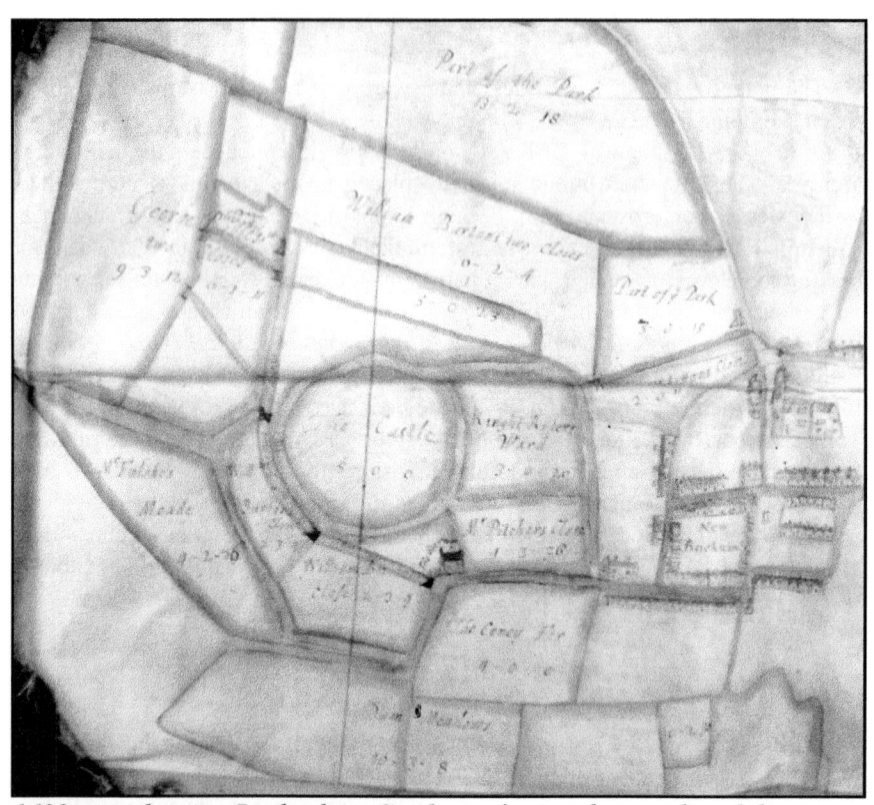

1693 map showing Buckenham Castle, its former deer park and the borough of New Buckenham.
Norfolk Record Office accn. Steele and Co. 23/9/86.

New Buckenham, a planned town at work 1530-1780

'It was as compact as a box of dominoes'
(Thomas Hardy, *Mayor of Casterbridge*, chapter IV).

Background and Sources

In the years 1530-1780 New Buckenham functioned as a very small borough and market town within the wood-pasture region of South Norfolk, not far from its western border with the less fertile Breckland.[1] It was a latecomer to the Norfolk scene, having been established by the first Earl William d'Albini as an adjunct to his new castle of Buckenham at some time between about 1146 and his death in 1176.[2] William planned his new town in a simple grid pattern on a spur of land rising a few metres above a western-flowing beck that eventually forms one of the head waters of the River Thet at Swangey Fen. New Buckenham is well known among historians as a medieval planned town whose layout and scale is largely unaltered.[3] William must have hoped it would flourish sufficiently to provide at least a market and craft centre to supply his castle, and the very large market place is an indication of his ambitions. These ambitions were balanced by the fact that in what was already a heavily settled landscape he was able to allot very little land to his new borough and was obliged in fact to borrow ground from the bishop in order to create a town field.[4]

So how did New Buckenham's beginnings as a borough and planned town with a large market place, but a very small land base, affect the way its economy functioned? In other words, how with such advantages and drawbacks did its inhabitants prosper in the sixteenth, seventeenth and eighteenth centuries? It may seem perverse to concentrate on the post-medieval history of a twelfth-century planned town, but in fact apart from a few key documents New Buckenham is sparsely recorded before about 1530 and abundantly thereafter. Evidence is assembled here down to about 1780.

1   B. Ayers, 'Medieval Planned Towns' in T. Ashwin and A. Davison eds, *An Historical Atlas of Norfolk* (Chichester, 2005), pp. 74-5.
2   P. Rutledge, 'Two Borough Charters', *Norfolk Archaeology* (hereafter *Norf. Arch.*), 43 (1999), pp. 313-17.
3   M.W. Beresford and J.K. St Joseph, *Medieval England, An Aerial Survey* (Cambridge, 1979), pp. 336-8.
4   F. Blomefield et al., *An Essay towards a Topographical History of the County of Norfolk* (1805-10 edn), I, pp. 383-4, 405.

After this the town seems to lose some of its urban functions. The market has declined, the borough organisation falters and the recording of property transfers at the borough court becomes haphazard. However, to round off the picture a population listing of 1803 is analysed (see Table H). Earlier records include landgable rentals 1542[5] and 1634 (b),[6] borough court books beginning in 1559 and continuing until the 1870s (a), high bailiffs' accounts 1550-1854 (b, c), series of town lawsuit papers from the 1560s to the 1630s mostly relating to disputes over commons (i), picture maps of 1597 and 1693, but no accurate large-scale survey until 1884,[7] and poor-law records from the 1680s onwards (f, g). The town has retained much of its sixteenth- and seventeenth-century housing stock (j, R).[8] Transfers of house property are regularly recorded in the borough court books and by combining this data with the 1634 landgable list, which is arranged topographically, the ownership history of each house can be reconstructed, often from the mid sixteenth century. In addition, between 1500 and 1780 there are about 220 New Buckenham wills and twenty-nine probate inventories, most of which can be related to specific properties.[9] Series of town trust and charity deeds between 1614 and 1759 are particularly useful in recording the occupations of leading inhabitants (e). However, few estate records of the Knyvetts, the d'Albinis' successors and resident lords of the borough until 1649, have survived so the extent to which the town's economy was bound up with that of the nearby castle is largely unknown.[10] It must have generated business for the market and inns as well as requiring bailiffs, park keepers, warreners and other servants.

By concentrating on those of known occupation among principal office-holders and property-owners (high bailiffs, trustees of charities and town lands, house owners and those for whom we have a will or a probate inventory) it is hoped to learn something of the economic life of the community, though women (except when they fall into the above

---

5   P. Rutledge, 'New Buckenham in 1542', *Norf. Arch.,* 45 (2007), pp. 222-31.
6   These lower-case letters within brackets refer to the Principal Sources listed on p. 98, as do references to Sources (a)-(k) in the notes.
7   Norfolk Record Office (hereafter NRO), MC 22/11; map in NRO, Steele & Co. 23/9/1986; O.S. 25 inch 1st edn sheets XCVI.5 and XCVI.9.
8   R: unpublished Reconstructions (see Principal Sources p. 98). For details of the housing stock see A. Longcroft ed., *The Historic Buildings of New Buckenham*, Journal of the Norfolk Historic Buildings Group 2 (Norwich, 2005).
9   The will dates given in the text are of making the will whereas those in the List of Wills and Administrations (pp.. 94-7) are of the year in which it was proved.
10   For the Knyvets see: R. Virgoe, 'The Earlier Knyvetts, the Rise of a Norfolk Gentry Family, part 2', *Norf. Arch.* 41 (1992), pp. 249-78; A. Hassell Smith, *County and Court, Government and Politics in Norfolk 1558-1603* (Oxford, 1974), pp. 52, 69; and B. Schofield ed., *The Knyvett Letters 1620-1644,* Norfolk Record Society (hereafter NRS) 20 (1949), p. 130.

BACKGROUND AND SOURCES

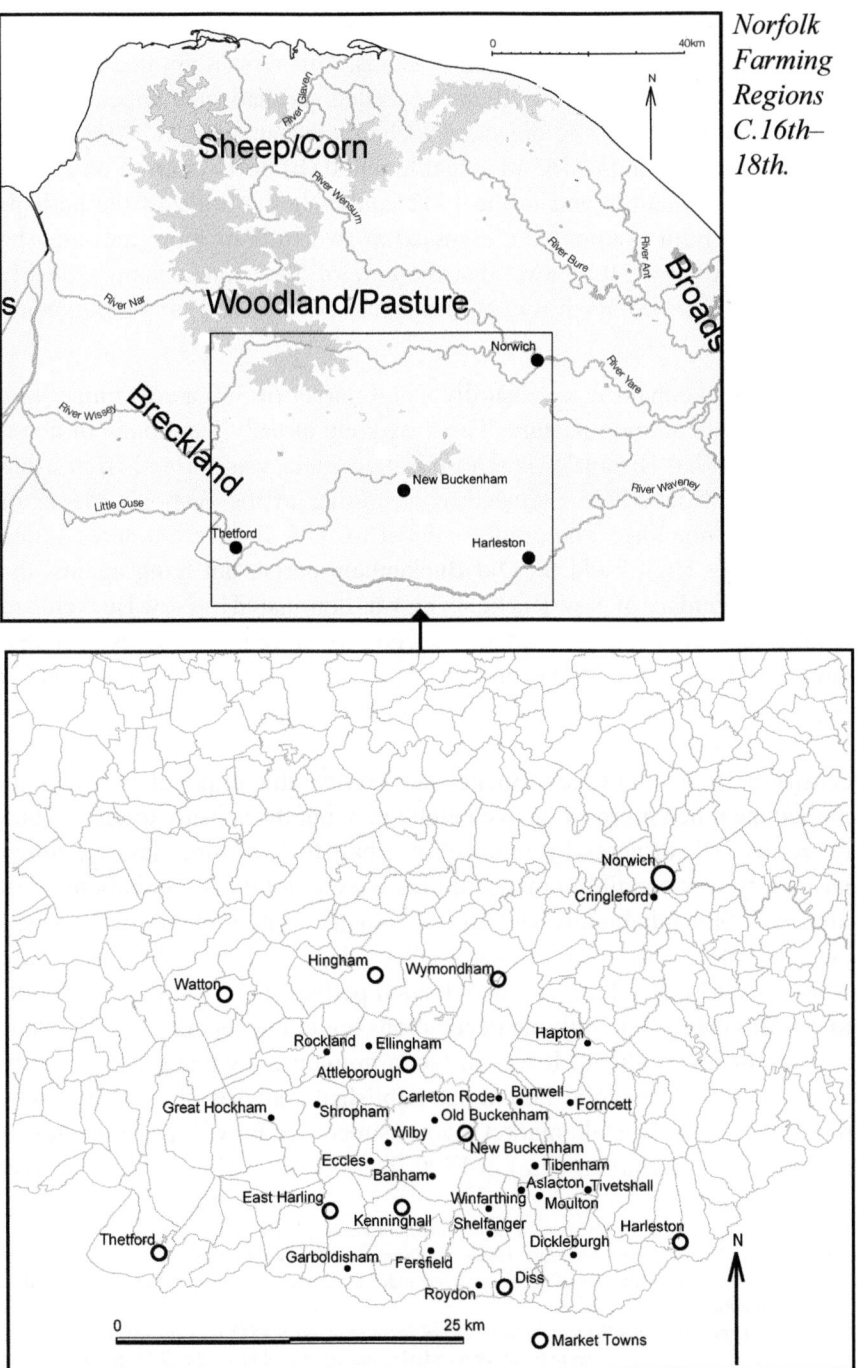

Fig. 1. New Buckenham regional setting and trade links.

categories) and the very poor are excluded by this approach. 'Major' house ownership is used as one criterion of status. This term is applied to houses that are or were three- rather than two-celled and had such appendages as shops, stallage rights and detached orchards and marshes. Of the eighty-one houses listed in the 1634 landgable rental (b) thirty (starred on Fig. 4) fall into this category and in the 1542 landgable list thirty of the perhaps seventy-six built holdings are assessed at two tofts or more and may be roughly equivalent. It follows that the elite of New Buckenham probably numbered no more than thirty families in the sixteenth and early seventeenth centuries.

New Buckenham is an absurdly small parish of 360 acres, ninety-five of which are common pasture. The town field already mentioned of about 180 acres called Bishop's Haugh or Haugh Field was formed from a big ditched enclosure that originated as an outlier of the Bishop's manor of Eccles and remained manorially subject to it. A further 190 acres called the Coole or High Field, in Old Buckenham parish but lying against the northern boundary of New Buckenham, was dominated by New Buckenham landowners and became in effect a second town field. 370 acres of arable land could not support the eighty or so households of the town and a population that communicant figures give as about 230 in 1578, 352 in 1603, 544 in 1676, and 637 in the detailed listing of 1803.[11] The Compton census of 1676 shows New Buckenham comparable in population with its immediate much more extensive neighbours, but the subsidy totals of 1663 reflect its lack of acres by rating it at a half to two thirds less.[12] Animal husbandry was certainly practised; pigs were ubiquitous[13] and about 1578 nineteen of the inhabitants paid tithe on a total of ninety-eight milch cows,[14] but nevertheless most families must have depended on full- or part-time work outside agriculture, and they tended perhaps less than the rural norm to conceal their often multiple occupations under the general description of yeoman or husbandman. It was in fact a miniature town and not a mainly agrarian settlement. John Pound has published analyses of occupations in nineteen leading Norfolk market towns as recorded in wills and inventories (effectively of the urban elite) in 1500-99, 1600-49 and 1650-99.[15] At New

11 NRO, PD 530/1; A. Whiteman ed., *The Compton Census of 1676* (1986), pp. cxx, 205; T.H. Bryant, *The Churches of Norfolk, Hundred of Shropham* (Norwich, 1913), p. 110; and NRO, MC 343/123(a). Multiples of 60% have been added to communicant figures to reach notional population totals.
12 R.M. Dunn ed., *Norfolk Lieutenancy Journal 1660-1676*, NRS 45 (1977), pp. 46, 51, 62.
13 For example, 29 owners were fined for wandering unringed pigs in 1542 and 21 in 1567 (Source a).
14 Tithe account among the New Buckenham parish papers.
15 J.F. Pound, *Tudor and Stuart Norwich* (Chichester, 1988), pp. 3-5.

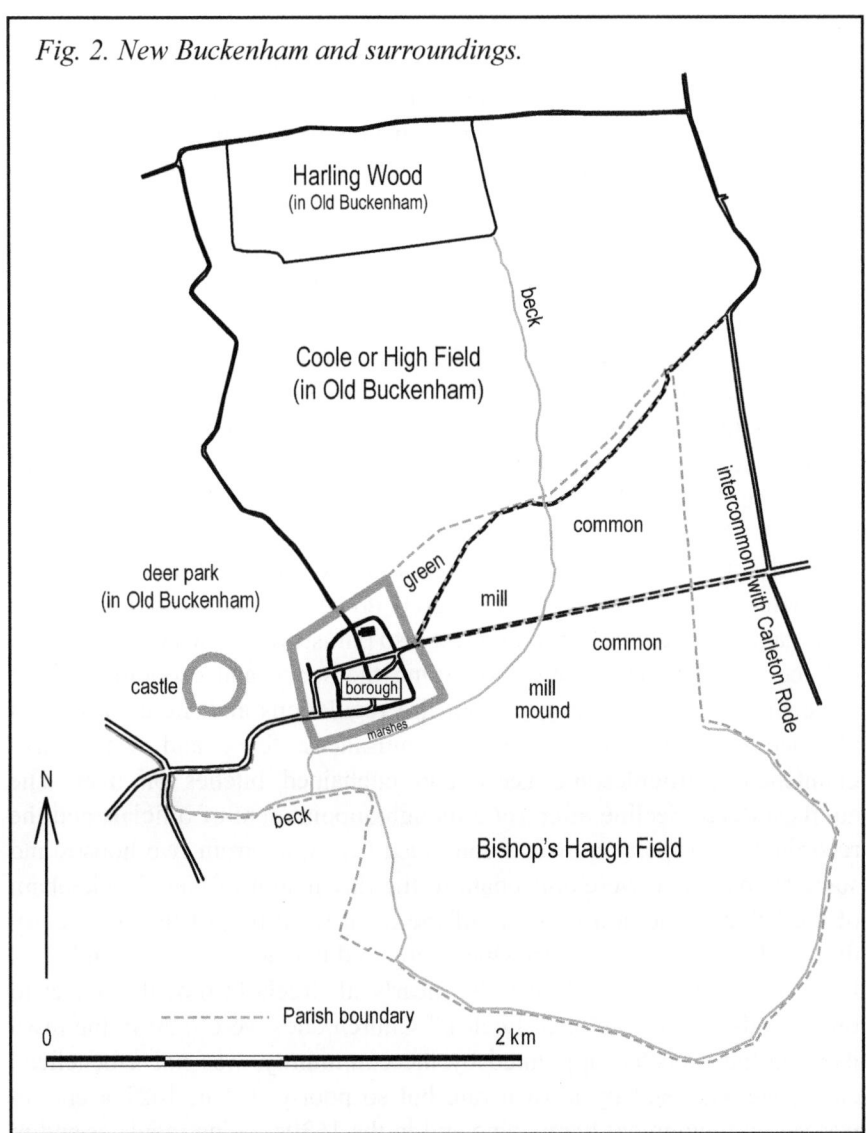

Fig. 2. New Buckenham and surroundings.

Buckenham (which is not among the nineteen) thirty-three of the fifty-six occupations listed are found at some time between 1500 and 1699, twenty-five of them consistently in 1500-99, in 1600-49, and in 1650-99 (see Table A). The figures for New Buckenham are drawn from all available sources, not solely from testamentary records, and there are eleven other trades that are too minor or too rural for John Pound's lists, but they do show an unexpectedly wide range of skills and opportunity. The elite have a narrower focus; esquire, gentleman, yeoman and husbandman apart, the known occupations of high bailiffs between 1550 and 1700 total fourteen and those of town and charity trustees between 1614 and 1759 eighteen (see Tables C and D). A borough organisation that maintained detailed regulation and documentation allows New Buckenham to be examined as a case-study of the way in which a small market town in Norfolk's wood-pasture region earned its living in the sixteenth to eighteenth centuries.

A low rateable value is not necessarily a disability and the town had certain other advantages over its more rural neighbours. Charters granted by the d'Albinis between 1176 and 1221 gave the burgesses personal freedom and ground rents (landgable) fixed at one halfpenny per tenement. They also gave the burgesses the right to hold their own borough courts.[16] By the 1560s these comprised a portman court, a general court with leet, and a market court. At the portman and general courts officials were appointed to oversee the simple borough organisation and acknowledgments were recorded of changes in house-ownership, validated by the payment of a small fine. The market court heard pleas arising from commercial transactions, but its records unfortunately do not specify the trade or parish of litigants. The general court and leet also punished by fine neighbourhood offences and passed byelaws governing the social and economic life of the community. These ranged from fire regulations and the exclusion of unwelcome immigrants to common nuisances, fence and watercourse maintenance, troublesome geese and unchained bitches on heat. The courts suffered decline after 1660 though appointment of officials and the recording of property transfers continued (a). Apart from two houses and some shops which were appendant to the tiny manor of New Buckenham of the Priory,[17] the houseowners of the town were free of the steep entry fines and other restrictions to which copyhold tenants were so often liable. Land in the Haugh Field was also nearly all freehold though subject to tithe payable to the rector of Eccles.[18] Church dues were light in the town itself as the minister, appointed by the community, was not a beneficed cleric. He was paid by a town rate but so poorly that in 1627 a charity was set up to augment his income and in the 1630s 'being menister and in wante' he was accounted for among the parish poor in need and sickness; even in 1716 the minister's rate only raised about £10.[19] Tithe, lactage and herbage were collected by the lord of the borough on animals, on orchards

16 Rutledge, 'Two Borough Charters', p. 315.
17 The National Archives (hereafter TNA) PRO, SP 5/3/10 and E 318/14/676.
18 NRO, MC 343/51 and DN/TER 60/2/1.
19 Eldred Charity account among parish papers; NRO, DN/TER 60/2/1 and MC 315/1-5. The minister's stipend was augmented by £10 per annum by a Commonwealth decree of 1656 – *Calendar of State Papers Domestic 1656-7*, p. 245.

and on the strip of marshland that ran south of the town, but in 1577-8 this totalled only 20s.10d.[20] Virtually every house carried a grazing right on the common; there were traditionally seventy-six to seventy-eight goings and in 1634 there were about eighty-seven houses.[21] In 1582 the inhabitants obtained exemption as tenants of ancient demesne from toll, liability to assize service and other centrally-imposed burdens.[22] Probably from 1546 and certainly from 1562 to at least 1622, profits arising from the letting of borough property–including the larger gildhall, which the town managed to retain at the Reformation, and the butchery–were earmarked for the discharge of subsidies levied on the inhabitants; it was stated during a lawsuit in 1622 'New Buckenham pay no taske, there being landes given for the payment thereof'.[23] In 1635 the leading townsman Charles Gostling calculated his yearly outgoings.[24] For his house (R4-5)[25] and orchard he paid 1d. landgable and 2d. herbage. For sixty acres of mostly enclosed meadow, pasture and arable land in the Haugh Field he paid 8s.9d. freehold rent, but 7s.1¼ d. for five acres of copyhold land. He was assessed at 8s.8d. for the minister's wages, and for his sixty-five acres in the field he paid 10d. per acre herbage to the parson of Eccles.

Since at least the thirteenth century the town had enjoyed a weekly market and a yearly fair.[26] A parish schoolmaster was endowed in 1646 and almshouses founded in 1491 and 1694 [27] added to the urban feel of the place as did the large market square with its tolhouse or market cross, stocks and whipping post, the publicly maintained church clock,[28] a gameplace on the green that had developed outside the east gate of the town,[29] and the closely-packed housing and the continuous frontages of the little place. Its position near a main crossroads and at the gate of the castle with its large if declining household encouraged marketing functions, brewing, innkeeping and associated trades, while the town moat and the nearby beck

20   Tithe account among New Buckenham parish papers.
21   In the landgable rental of 1634 (Source b) 81 houses are listed and about 6 more were free of landgable. Compare the perhaps 80 built properties listed in 1542 (Rutledge, 'New Buckenham in 1542', p. 226) and the 89 houses in 1777 (NRO, DN/VIS 28/2).
22   NRO, MC 22/1.
23   Trust deeds of town lands 1562-1604 among parish papers; suit papers 1622 in Source (i).
24   NRO, MC 343/51.
25   These 'R' references refer to properties mentioned in the Reconstructions. The position of the houses is shown on Fig. 4.
26   Blomefield, *History of Norfolk* (1805-10 edn), I, pp. 395-6.
27   Will of John Verdon, 1491; copy will of William Barber, 1694. The references to these and other wills mentioned are given on pp. 94-7. In 1726 the schoolmaster was required to be expert in grammar, arithmetic and fitness of writing and the town promised him 'suitable encouragement' above his salary– *Norwich Gazette* 11-18/6/1726.
28   High Bailiff's account 1568 in Source (c).
29   See Source (a), 1566.

brought water for tanning to the backyards of houses and carried away the waste products of brewing and dyeing. The market place was narrowed in the 1470s by building over its southern section a line of high-quality oriel-windowed houses. R81 is dendro-dated 1473 and R83 documented from 1478-9.[30] There is little evidence from the medieval period, but there is just enough to show a pattern of employment that persisted after 1530. Occupational surnames in 1306 include tailor, litster (dyer), currier, sutor (shoemaker), lorimer (harness-maker) and chapman, as well as blacksmith, locksmith, carpenter and reeder.[31] In 1455 two aliens, who may have taken English surnames from their trades, were Hugh Shoemaker and Peter Tayllor.[32]

Analysis of wills, town land and charity trust deeds (referred to hereafter as town trusts), the known occupations of the annually-chosen high bailiffs, and property reconstructions show that the distinctively New Buckenham trades in 1530-1780 were cloth finishing and sale, leather production and working, butchering, innkeeping, brewing and baking, and the business of grocer/apothecary. From 1704-5 to 1715-16 poor rate lists survive which include valuations of stock in trade. Innkeepers and butchers do not figure probably because their investment was in real estate rather than stock, but three woollendrapers head the lists and next come the tanners, then the grocers, then the bakers. There was one relatively highly-rated brewer and one brazier. Seven other trades including one woman milliner are at the lowest valuation. The title Mr is accorded only to the drapers, tanners and grocers, and to the brewer. A thinner list of 1750 shows a similar hierarchy (see Tables E to G).

The Market (see Fig. 3)

Before examining specific trades the market must be referred to. Unlike the estate-orientated marketing system discerned as a regular feature in the sheep-corn region,[33] New Buckenham in the less squire-dominated wood-pasture was firmly within an economy centred on the market place. The New Buckenham market place must have been reorganised when the southern part was built over in the 1470s and again after 1715 when the market cross was moved from the north-west quarter to its present, more central, position. The new cross is probably part of an attempt at refurbishment in the face of decline, however; Blomefield said in 1739 that the market was of late years

30   Longcroft, *Historic Buildings*, pp. 193 and NRO, Rye 84.
31   *Calendar of Close Rolls 1302-7*, pp. 475-6.
32   N.J.M. Kerling, 'Aliens in Norfolk 1436-1485', *Norf. Arch.* 33 (1963), pp. 200-15.
33   A. Hassell Smith, 'Labourers in Late Sixteenth Century England, a Case Study from North Norfolk, *Continuity and Change* 4 (3) (1989), p. 378.

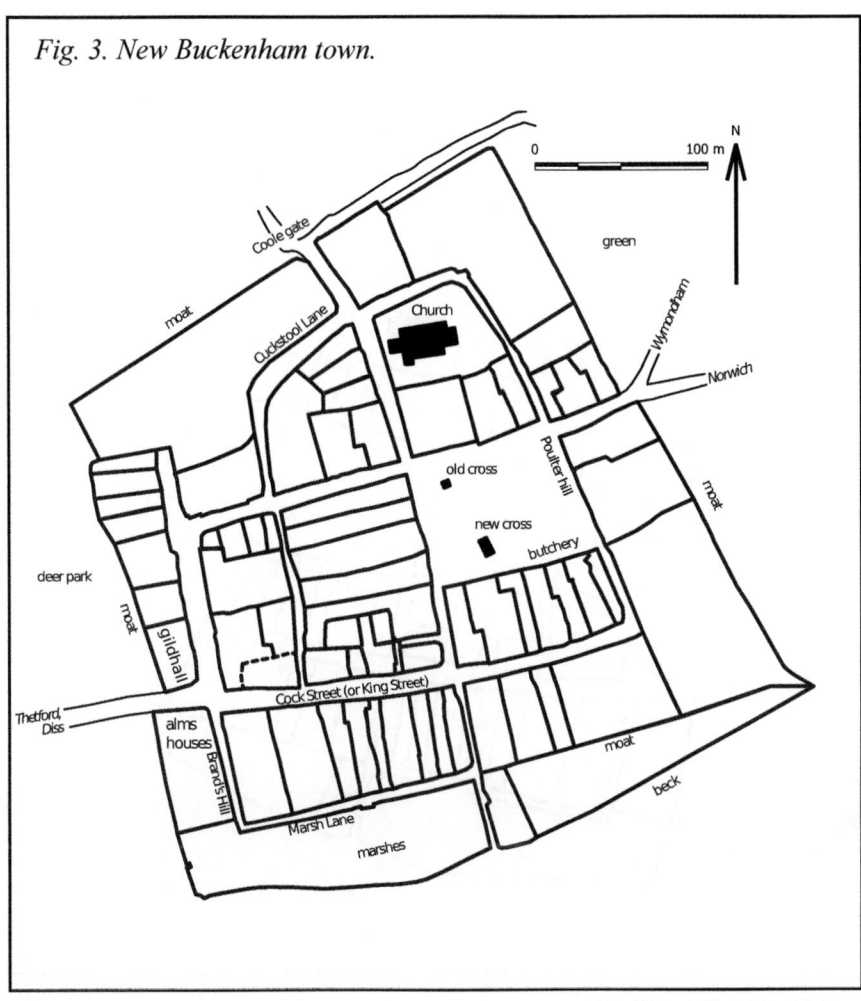

Fig. 3. New Buckenham town.

much decayed.[34] In the sixteenth century the area was already obstructed by shops and other permanent encroachments; so much so that by the 1560s the green had developed outside the east gate and by the 1590s the fair had spilled onto it.[35] The landgable rental of 1542 lists within the market square one messuage with stalls and standings, two messuages with shops, and three houses and various other messuages with shops and stalls; there was also a forge and a tavern (d). In 1595 and later shops are described with upper chambers (the loft of the present market cross is in fact reconstructed from two of them) (a, j). In 1679 one stood between other shops and a

34 For narrowing of the market place see Longcroft, *Historic Buildings*, p. 40, NRO, BL/R 19 and Rye 84. For new cross conveyances of 1715 and 1752 see parish papers and for the market's decline Blomefield, *History of Norfolk* (1805-10 edn), I, pp. 396-7
35 NRO, PD 254/172 and Beresford and St Joseph, *Aerial Survey*, pp. 226-8.

*Fig. 4. Reconstructions.
The numbers follow the route taken by the 1634 Landgable collectors: major houses are marked *.*

shared staircase gave access to a secure chamber above–one of a row of two-storied commercial premises.[36] A drawing of 1820 in private possession shows unexpected sophistication in a seventeenth-century shop behind the market cross with awning and oriel upper window.[37] A reference of 1627 to shops or workshops further describes them; they may have functioned as wholesale and retail outlets as well as workshops and warehouses (a). (The occupation of shopkeeper, which implies a retail outlet not tied to a specific

36   Conveyance among parish papers.
37   P. Rutledge, 'New Buckenham in 1820' in S. Ashley and A. Marsden eds, *Landscapes and Artefacts* (Archaeopress, 2014), p. 232.

THE MARKET

trade, is not found until 1772 (R35)). Other shops were sited in the houses round the market place. The market focused the trade of the town into this congested area. The town bushel was chained under the cross, the stocks were close by, and the scales were similarly secured in the nearby church.[38] Sixteenth- and seventeenth-century sources show that it was above all a provision and leather market with butchers', fish and poultry, and also shoemakers' stalls.[39] Meat, often on the hoof, butter, cheese, eggs, corn, malt and timber came in. In 1542 there were thirty stalls and later thirty-one. The butchery proper formed three sides of a square open to the west, the seven stalls on the eastern side being described as the 'new house' in 1542 and as 'double' in 1559, while eleven on the south side were called the long stalls. To the north and south stood a line of lesser (outsetters') stalls usually hired by the day while the rest were let out by the year. The butchery was thatched, paved with cobbles and gravel and drained by a gutter. The number of stalls does not necessarily reflect the number of butchers. Some hired two or even three stalls; some stalls were unlet; and the daily stalls were only hired intermittently. An early seventeenth-century account records nineteen yearly lettings, but ten to twelve is the usual number. Even so the meat market was of an impressive size. It seems to have been cleared away by about 1763.[40] The poultry market, *pulter hylle* in 1542, is located by abuttals on the eastern edge of the market place. It was still active in 1634, but all memory of it seems lost by 1713 when it was called Boulter Hill, no doubt with reference to bolting or sifting of meal in the oatmill at nearby R46. The fish market, documented from 1566, lay north of the butchery but in 1603 and 1640 it had been displaced by shoemakers' stalls. The fishmongers relocated, however, and their stalls are last referred to in the 1720s.[41] The preservation of fish and flesh and the making of butter and cheese required salt[42] and the salters are recorded just once, in 1569, when ordered not to stand with their stalls under the – no doubt jettied out–ends of Roger Dade's and Peter Clarke's shops. Lesser traders stood between fixtures; in 1578 Dade and two other shop owners were accused of exacting toll from persons standing near their shops but in the open market.

Retail trade was confined to the market place and the town authorities were concerned to make it attractive and prevent unfair trading and profiteering. Byelaws of about 1559 direct the sub-bailiff to sweep the

---

38 Source (a), 1637.
39 Unless otherwise stated, the remainder of this paragraph and the next are based on Source (a) before 1660, and Sources (b), (c) and (d).
40 NRO, MC 343/11-12.
41 NRO, DN/TER 33/1/3.
42 P. Basing, *Trades and Crafts in Medieval Manuscripts* (British Library, 1990), p. 86.

Fig. 5.1-5.11. Location of trades.

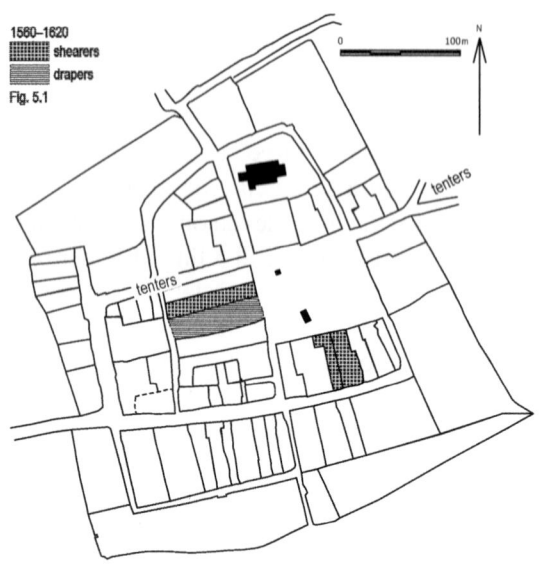

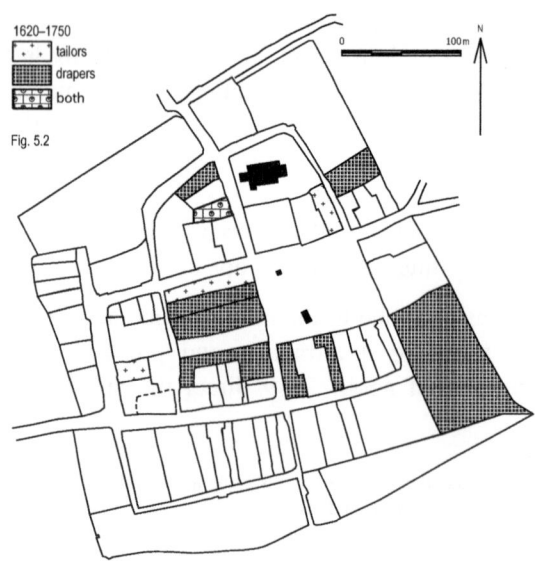

The Market

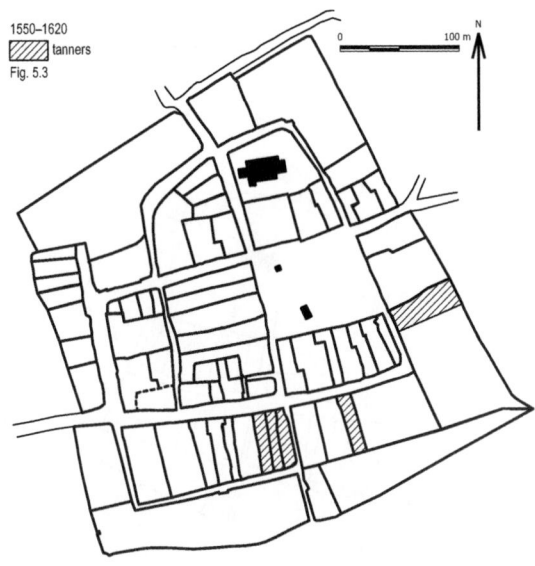

1550–1620
tanners
Fig. 5.3

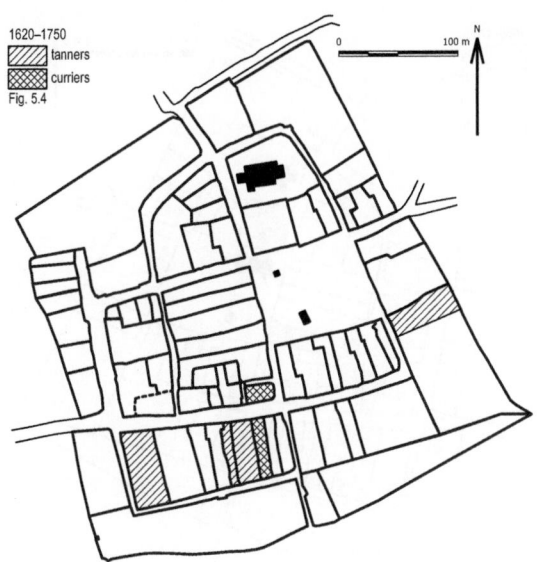

1620–1750
tanners
curriers
Fig. 5.4

22 NEW BUCKENHAM A PLANNED TOWN AT WORK 1530-1780

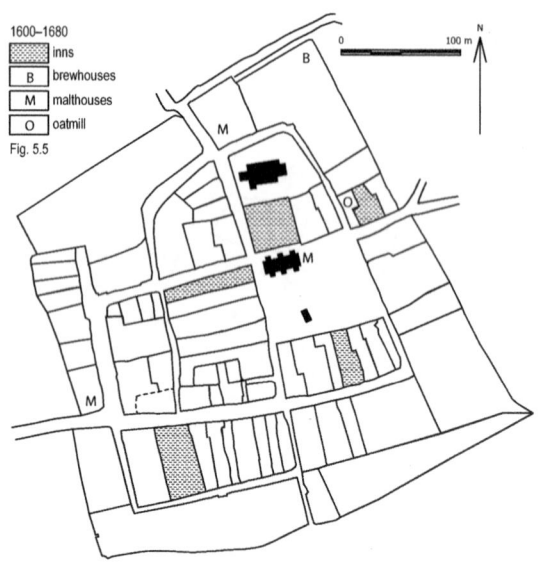

Fig. 5.5

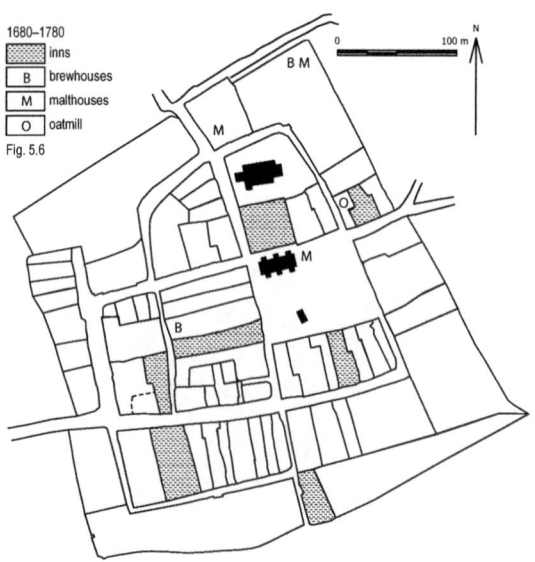

Fig. 5.6

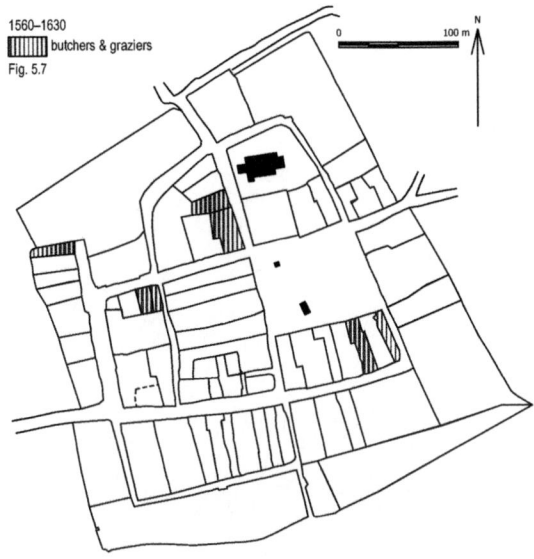

1560–1630
butchers & graziers
Fig. 5.7

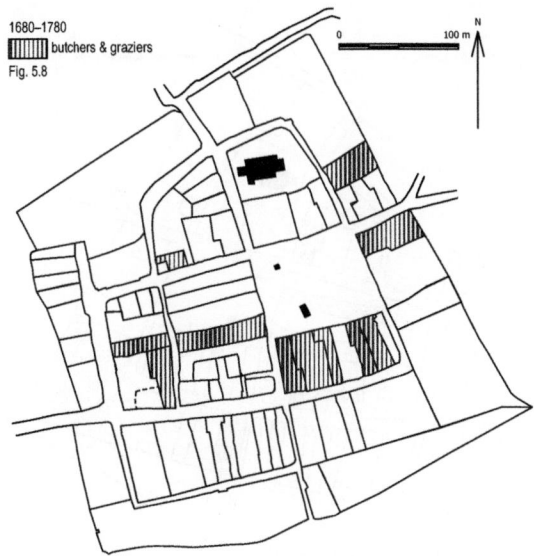

1680–1780
butchers & graziers
Fig. 5.8

1680–1780
grocers & apothecaries
physicians & surgeons
both
Fig. 5.9

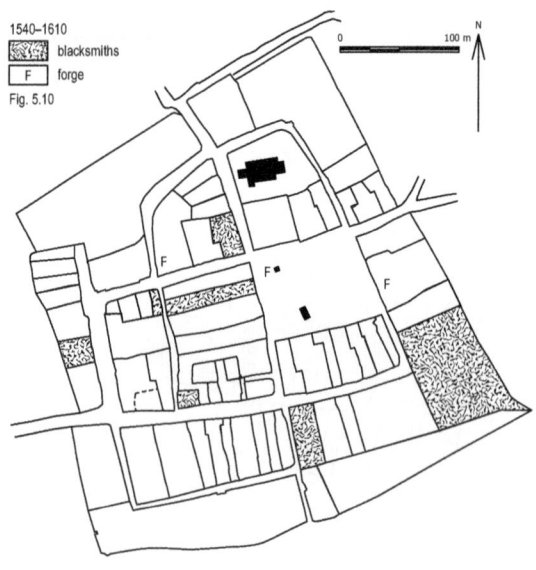

1540–1610
blacksmiths
F forge
Fig. 5.10

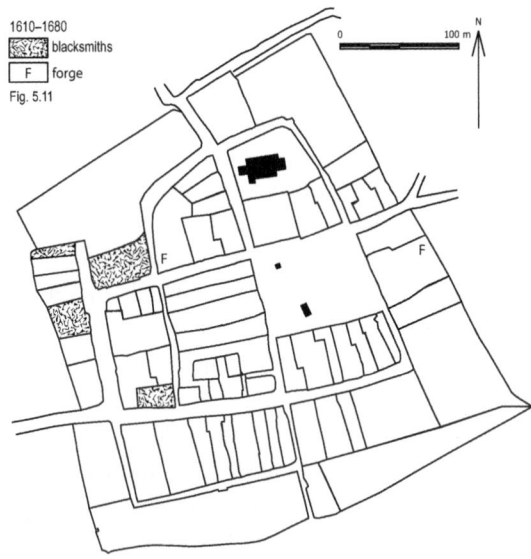

Fig. 5.11
1610–1680
blacksmiths
F forge

market place weekly and to eject pigs found there, and in 1613 Francis Dickerson was fined for emptying urine from his chamber windows to the harm of neighbours and of others coming to market. In 1564 it was ordered that no-one should clean their place before market day and throw the dirt into the street. In 1566 no baker was to buy grain called *yoynt* (perhaps mixed grain) save in the market and no brewer was to buy malt similarly. In 1601 Robert Myller was accused of intercepting by the wayside stranger merchants coming to market with butter and other things and Robert Hubbard of Harling allowed his wife to do the same, to the oppression of the poor. To prevent such pre-emption it was ordered in 1567-8 that brewers were not to buy malt nor bakers winter corn before 1 pm and in 1570 no kiddier (hawker or huckster) was to buy butter, cheese or eggs before 2 pm, and there are presentments for forestalling rye and malt before the time set, to the grave oppression of the poor (1614). Butchering was also controlled. Butchers were fined for killing pigs in the street (1562; slaughtering was confined to the market place where the condition of the animals was presumably checked) and there are a number of presentments for selling bad meat, infected pork and beef and the flesh of pregnant or out-of-condition ewes. However an order of 1578 that no-one was to let his pigs lie at night in the butchers' stalls implies that hygiene was basic. Quality control was in the hands of the searchers of flesh and fish whose numbers varied between the three and two respectively appointed in 1563 and one for flesh and one for fish in 1632. Regulation of the leather trade and of baking and brewing are described below.

In South Norfolk within a twelve-mile radius of New Buckenham a pattern of market days was established: Monday Kenninghall, Tuesday East Harling, Wednesday Harleston and Watton, Thursday Attleborough, Friday Diss and Wymondham, and Saturday Thetford and New Buckenham.[43] In the sixteenth and seventeenth centuries when the borough court books and high bailiffs' accounts (principal sources a, c) have relevent if haphazard records of presentments made and butchers' stalls hired, traders are known to have brought goods or animals to New Buckenham from all but one (Harleston) of these towns, and they also came from non-market villages within the area. Table B shows the years in which individual traders hired stalls and/or were fined, not the total number of traders coming in. The figures are too incomplete to generalise much from, but the number of bakers from Wymondham in 1563-85 is notable as is their later decline. Some of the external bakers may have brought a more sophisticated product than New Buckenham produced, though the town could muster a gingerbread-maker in 1638.[44] The number of butchers is reflected in the size of the meat market; they came regularly from Diss, Kenninghall and Carleton Rode and (before 1585) Garboldisham and intermittently from fourteen other places. Their absence from the Breckland villages to the west is noticeable as is the absence of traders in general from the Norwich-dominated area to the east beyond Hapton and Wymondham, though one leading Norwich tradesman, the grocer Robert Craske, had property, R24, in New Buckenham in 1625-34 as did Richard Kett a Norwich mercer (R22) in 1630 and a maltster from Cringleford by Norwich, Thomas Cubitt, owned R14 in 1623-31. They may have traded in the town.[45]

The Cloth Trade (see Figs 5.1-2)

A major industry of the town, the emphasis was on finishing and sale rather than manufacture. Only one worstead weaver, Peter Craske, ever became a town trustee and only one weaver, the darnick weaver Robert

43 David Dymond, 'Medieval and Later Markets' in Ashwin and Davison, *Historical Atlas,* pp. 76-7 and Emanuel Bowen's mid-18th century *Accurate map of Norfolk,* which records market days.
44 TNA PRO, E 178/5534.
45 B. Cozens-Hardy and E.A. Kent, *The Mayors of Norwich 1403-1835* (Norwich, 1938), p. 75; P. Millican ed., *The Register of the Freemen of Norwich 1548-1713* (Norwich, 1934), pp. 102-3, 232.

Meene, high bailiff (b, e). Weavers do occur, whether of linen or wool or both is not always clear. Three are recorded between 1569 and 1578 including John Smith (R40) who made a window into his neighbour's yard, perhaps to light his loom (a). Later come the darnick weaver Robert Meene (R43; will 1664) and Peter Craske 1694 (R41) and Francis Buxton 1734 (R1), worstead weavers. Edward Rudland (R33) took a parish apprentice as a worstead weaver in 1694.[46] Six worstead weavers, otherwise unrecorded, appear between 1694 and 1786 in the poor law papers (g). A few woolcombers also occur. Robert Norman woolcomber leased a stable from the town in 1633 and owned a cottage (on R31) from 1629. He was described as a husbandman in 1654[47] and in his will two years later. One woolcomber in 1685 and two woolcombers and hosiers in 1778 and 1783 appear in the poor law papers (g). The woolcomber/hosiers must have processed the raw wool and organised its spinning and knitting into stockings. Such spinning was probably done by women. Two witnesses in the tobacco suit in 1638 (below pp. 72-3), one aged about 32 and the other about 35, are described as spinsters and that this was their occupation rather than their status is indicated by a reference to another witness as a single woman. A painter, Stephen Stacye, left his wife a clock reel, a device used by spinners to fix the length of yarn in a skein, in 1634. One hosier, John Rushmer, who followed Norman at R31, was prosperous enough to be rated on stock in 1712-13 to 1715-16, though at the lowest valuation (f). Hemp processing is evidenced by an order of 1599 that no inhabitant should soak hemp on any pit on the common (a). This may imply hempen cloth or rope production. Gage the knacker (ropemaker) supplied ropes for the town well in the 1630s (b). Linen weavers appear later as the South Norfolk linen industry expanded.[48] They include John Briting (will 1667), Henry Blyth (will 1711), Robert Stone (R33; died 1763), William Grey (R75; will 1759), John Reynolds (R13; town trustee in 1759 (k)), and John Edwards (R66-7) in 1765 (a). Stone and Edwards had sizeable houses, Edwards sported the alternative title of gentleman, and Stone must be related to Robert Stone minister of New Buckenham 1718-39. The parish census of 1803 lists one undifferentiated weaver, one worstead weaver and four linen weavers (see Table G).

More important than cloth production were cloth finishing in the sixteenth century and cloth selling in the seventeenth and early eighteenth. The Miles and Warden families used the specialised crafts of dyeing and

---

46   Source (g); house no. R31.
47   Source (h).
48   N. Evans, *The East Anglian Rural Linen Industry: Rural Industry and Local Economy 1500-1850* (Aldershot, 1985), *passim*.

shearing for nearly a century. From 1566 to 1598 members of both familes are fined in various combinations for maintaining tenters (cloth-stretching frames) on the common; these are shown on the 1597 map[49] (see Fig. 5.1). The only other known tenters were presented in 1597 as set up at a backstreet crossroads within the town (a). William Miles in his will of 1534 left his son Robert a pair of shearman's shears and a great cauldron to be delivered when he set up as a dyer. Robert Warden's will of 1591 directed that after his death his son John should occupy the shop and dyehouse, but if he displeased his mother he was to have shears and shearboards only. His inventory lists in his shop five pairs of shearman's shears and a dyeing copper.[50] John Miles was the last of this line. Described as a shearman in 1606 and at the time of his death (and as a yeoman in 1609),[51] his will of 1615 does not indicate much prosperity, but the Miles' and Wardens' houses (R53, R83, R84) were buildings of status. His widow on selling the reversion of R83 in 1616 covenanted payments to six children of the late John Warden shearman.[52] One later shearman is Francis Fisher (R60; will 1694), a man of moderate means. Like shearing, the use of tenters implies that the cloth being processed was fulled rather than worstead.[53] No indication has been found of a fulling mill at New Buckenham, but for a small-scale industry fulling troughs in the dyers' and shearers' workshops may have sufficed.[54] However, in an extent of the possessions of Old Buckenham Priory made in the mid 1530s, Robert Mene fuller of Harleston is listed as lessee for a term of 99 years beginning in 1533 of two shops lying together in New Buckenham.[55] They were probably on the south side of the market place and he still had them in 1542 (d). It is likely that in the 1530s and 1540s at least cloth was fulled at Harleston and brought to New Buckenham to be further processed, warehoused and sold.

Vendors rather than makers and finishers of cloth, the drapers and mercers appear in the second half of the sixteenth century. They were an interrelated group generally of leading tradesmen rising into the minor gentry. In Norwich the mercers concentrated on finer wares especially silks, and the drapers on woollen cloth, mixed fabrics such as the furnishing material dornix or darnick and linens.[56] In less-regulated New Buckenham the same men often went by both descriptions, though one silkman, presumably a

49　NRO, MC 22/11.
50　NRO, DN/INV 8/33.
51　Will of Richard Sturdevant, 1606; deed of 1609 among parish papers.
52　Deed among parish papers.
53　U. Priestly, *The Fabric of Stuffs* (UEA, 1990) p. 7.
54　H. Swanson, *Medieval Artisans* (Oxford, 1989), p. 41.
55　TNA PRO, SP 5/3/10.
56　U. Priestley and A. Fenner, *Shops and Shopkeepers in Norwich* (UEA, 1985), pp. 23-4.

greater specialist, is recorded. John Payne mercer is listed as a tithingman in 1568-9 and another John Payne is similarly recorded as tailor and draper between 1568 and 1583 (a). He supplied hose for one of the parish poor in 1589 (c). One branch of the leading Tendall or Kendall family was among other things drapers. William Tendall who bought R55 in 1557 is called yeoman in 1566 and in his will of 1580, but he refers in his will to a warehouse and shop at New Buckenham and a shop at East Harling. His son John was a draper aged about 35 in 1596, but is more grandly called merchant or mercer when he entered his son Richard at Caius College, Cambridge, in 1615.[57] He is styled linendraper in 1616 and woollendraper in his will of 1625.[58] He enlarged his house plot (R55) and probably rebuilt and set back the house in the late 1590s but his will indicates declining prosperity. He refers to a partnership with his son John in selling corn, and directs that his assets should be put towards the payment of his legacies and John's debts. They had also diversified into timber as in 1624 they were rated for over sixty acres of woodland, including Harling Wood, nearby but in Old Buckenham, and John was defendant in a market court plea about three loads of timber in 1630. A shop, R54, lying on the market place opposite the house had since 1599 been converted from a forge. Shortly before his death John passed this to another son, Henry, a town trustee in 1627 (e), described as both draper and mercer between 1627 and 1633.[59]

Henry Kendall's shop was bought in 1627 by John Gooch (R40, R48f), who was documented as a mercer and woollendraper between 1627 and 1650; he was also a town trustee. By 1669 he had assumed the style of gentleman and retired to Carleton Forehoe. John Gooch junior, also a town trustee, is recorded as a woollendraper in 1669 and in his will of 1680. He also used the title of gentleman.[60] His bequest of a house in Carleton Rode to Thomas Cuson weaver of Hockley Hole near London may indicate kin or trade links with the capital. His son Stephen (active 1680-1704, will dated 1703) is called both woollendraper and gentleman from 1693.[61] The will refers to messuages and shops in New and Old Buckenham and East Harling. The will of a kinsman, Stephen Gooch yeoman, dated 1690 gives a taste of the family's wealth and status. He had property in eight parishes and bequeathed gold and silver objects and books of which his wife was to have six but 'not exceeding quartos'. However this Stephen was probably a

57 NRO, PD 254/172; J. and J.A. Venn, *Alumni Cantabrigiensis part 1* (Cambridge, 1922-27), vol. 3, p. 7; deed of 1616 among parish papers.
58 NRO, Pomeroy 30/8/95, Old Buckenham rate list 1624.
59 Will of Osborne Stacye, 1633; Sources (a) and (e).
60 John was defendant in a market court plea about two loads of timber in 1637 – NRO, MC 22/9; Sources (a) and (e); will of Anne Dawes, 1662-3.
61 Sources (a), (e) and (f).

steward or bailiff not a draper.[62] A kinsman, John Knyvett worstead weaver of Fundenhall, was supervisor of several Gooch wills and was perhaps a business associate.

The Gooches were dissenters, as witness John's 'fiduciall resignation' in his will of 1680 of his soul 'into the hands of the father of spirits and into the bosome of my deare lord Jesus' and his bequest to poor ministers, and his wife Frances' legacy of 1698 to the Congregation at Wymondham 'to which I belong'. The last Gooch to trade at New Buckenham was Thomas, woollendraper and town trustee in 1723, who supplied burying cloths (required by law to be of wool) for paupers in 1695-6 (e, f).

A succession of drapers followed the Wardens at R84. First came Charles Nunn, woollendraper in 1611 and 1614, who died in 1618. He was succeeded by another Charles, town trustee and woollendraper in 1627 (e), who sold up in 1641 and retired to Larling. Jointly concerned in the sale, perhaps as a kinsman or partner, was Thomas Colman woollendraper of Diss who was a New Buckenham town trustee in 1627. William Wade was the purchaser, also a town trustee, who occurs as a woollendraper 1641-61 and a gentleman 1661-2.[63] His will of 1664 reverts to woollendraper and refers to shops in unnamed parishes and property in South Lopham, East Harling and Winfarthing. Robert his son was a woollendraper and town trustee in 1669 (e) and a 'comer' (a woolcomber) in the parish register in 1664. After 1693 R84 passed to Richard Crowe, woollendraper in 1687 (g) but called gentleman on his armorial tombstone in 1717.[64] He had three shops in New Buckenham and as a woollendraper had the highest assessment for stock in 1705-6 to 1715-16 (f).

The Kendall house R55 was bought by Edward Warne in 1632. He was also a town trustee and occurs as a woollendraper from 1641 to when he made his will in 1652 (e).[65] In 1643-4 he bought up the green broadcloth that religious changes had removed from the communion table, and the minister's discarded surplice (b). He left property in six parishes and pecuniary bequests of £1200, and his daughter Rebecca included a baronet, Sir Francis Bickley, among her four husbands.[66] In addition he owned the Three Feathers Inn (R83). The sizeable house R41 also passed through clothing families. Formerly Charles Nunn's, in 1634 it belonged to Thomas

62   NRO, DS 514.
63   Source (e); will of Richard Pereson, 1611. William Wade died while serving as high bailiff: Source (a).
64   NRO, MS 1243; Blomefield, *History of Norfolk* (1805-10 edn), I, p. 404.
65   Source (b), 1643-4; Blomefield, *History of Norfolk* (1805-10 edn), I, p. 402.
66   Sources (e) 1641, (a) 1654, (g) and (b).

Colman (e). Robert Wade sold it in 1674 and in 1687-96 it belonged to Peter Craske, already noted as a worstead weaver.

The Shermans were a less successful family. John Sherman, draper, was in business by 1611 when his shop on the market place is mentioned (a). His son John inherited R57-8, a major house with a detached shop on the market; he was woollendraper and town trustee in 1627 (e). In 1630 he was accused of haunting taverns night and day (a). In 1639, probably to evade debt, he enlisted in the King's army against the rebel Scots; his neighbour at R59, Thomas Lincoln, went with him (a).[67] He turned the property over to his brother William in 1648 and took to the more congenial occupation of selling ale and probably also malting (a). William is documented as a silkman aged about 26 in 1638 and is again described as a silkman in his will of 1659.[68] He survived to sell the house in 1650 but kept the shop and he had a sideline as a tapster (a).

Almost the last and one of the most obviously prosperous of the New Buckenham drapers was Thomas Blake (R4-5, R86). He was in business as a woollendraper by 1705 (f) and when he made his will in 1739. He also sold fine linen since the town bought ten yards of hollands from him for a surplice in 1715. His grave slab gives him the alternative title of mercer. The will shows that he had rebuilt his house and mentions his wife's jointure of £1000. Fulcher his son enjoyed gentry status and inherited a property, R4-5, that with its long pond formed from a length of the town moat and its ornamental garden house was clearly a place of leisure.[69] Richard Curteis was rated for stock in 1750. He seems to have been a tenant of Fulcher Blake's at R86 and had probably taken over the business. He died shortly after.[70] The very last draper found, Richard Clarke, was a town trustee in 1759 (k).

Interrelationships between the leading cloth families are illuminated unexpectedly in the accounts they rendered as high bailiffs. In 1628-9 Henry Kendall refers to his 'cozen' Charles Nunn, in 1643-4 Edward Warne to his 'brother' Gooch, in 1644-5 William Wade to his 'cousins' Rowett (grocer) and Gooch, and in 1682 Henry Meene to his 'cousins' John Barber jun. and Gooch (c). (Meene was the son of the darnick weaver and the Barbers were butchers).

67 NRO, MC 22/9.
68 TNA PRO, E178/5534. A deed among the parish papers documents the descent of the shop from John Sherman to John and William his sons. William made his will as William Sherman.
69 Churchwardens' accounts among parish papers, under date 1715. Thomas Blake's grave slab is in New Buckenham church. For the house and garden layout see Blomefield, *History of Norfolk* (1739-75 edn), I, p. 246, and a map in private possession.
70 Source (f).

Tailors, makers of garments rather than suppliers of cloth, were lesser men[71]–only one became high bailiff for example–though John Payne had been noted as both tailor and draper in 1568-83, and John Miles, tailor, who in 1602 owned the lesser house R29 must be related to the Miles family of shearmen. The poor law papers show only one draper, Philip Brown in 1688, who took a parish apprentice, whereas four tailors occur among the minor tradesmen and journeymen whom these papers mainly document (g). A New Buckenham tailor, John Pyknett, was in the Fleet Prison in 1569 for non-appearance in a plea of account,[72] but William Lambard tailor fared better and inherited the major house R81 in 1573.[73] John Hubbert is recorded as a tailor in his probate inventory of 1592.[74] John Dowghty inherited R39 in 1631. Tailor and infant school keeper, he figures in an Exchequer suit in 1638 as an illicit tobacco vendor (below, pp. 72-3). In 1654 Nicholas Richardson, tailor, was established by Henry Norman in a small new inset house at R31, on condition of maintaining his son, the child of Norman's sister Jane. Members of the Smyth family made clothes for the poor in the late 1690s and 1713-14 (f) and about 1706 John Smyth, tailor, left the Wealden house R49 to his son John, also a tailor. Three other tailors were testate. Thomas Denny's will of 1677 refers to property in Wymondham including a (sublet) woolcombing house but his inventory totals only £7.13s.4d at New Buckenham.[75] John Ince made his brief will in 1684, which is of interest because the preamble shows him to have been of the same Dissenting persuasion as the Gooches, and his two-celled house R40 had previously been owned by them. Edward Hagon or Hacon whose will is dated 1720 owned the major house R53 from 1695. One merchant-tailor (that is, a tailor who supplied the cloth he made up into clothes), Richard Stepney, owned R69 and is among those rated lowest in the stock-in-trade lists in 1704-5 to 1706-7, as is one woman, Elizabeth Kinge, milliner, in 1704-5 to l712-13 (f).

Other clothing trades include the hatters. Francis Marjoram or Margeries occurs as a hatter in 1578 and about 1590.[76] William Andrewes, hatter, had a stall or standing at Buckenham fair about 1563 when he was in dispute with a Norwich merchant about a consignment of black felt hats.[77] He owned R50 and made his will as a haberdasher in 1576 leaving hats, caps,

71 Priestly and Fenner, *Shops and Shopkeepers,* pp. 23-4.
72 *Calendar of Patent Rolls 1566-9,* p. 390.
73 Described as a tailor in Source (i), 1562.
74 NRO, DN/INV 9/216.
75 NRO, DN/INV 60B/26.
76 Source (a) and tax list c. 1590 among parish papers.
77 W. Rye ed., *Depositions taken before the Mayor and Aldermen of Norwich* (Norwich, 1905), p. 80.

hose and wool in his shop. The house was sold on his death by his son Thomas, a chandler at Edmonton in Middlesex. Robert Turner's trade almost defies definition. His ill-written probate inventory of 1592 includes, besides haberdashery, ironmongery, groceries, spices, dyes, and a whole range of other goods from soap to rat poison and from frankincense to sugar candy.[78] He made and sold candles and cheese and there was a linen shop. In what seems to have been virtually a lock-up shop at East Harling he concentrated on haberdashery and drapery and here he kept his stall gear. It is no surprise to find him from 1571 onwards supplying the town with items as diverse as a maypole, swords for the town militiamen and a book, Musculus' *Commonplaces*.[79] In the 1620s the Clarke family lived at nearby Carleton Rode but traded at New Buckenham. As early as 1542 they owned a complex (R77-79) in the middle of the market place, described in 1627-8 as a house with three shops with chambers above and stalls adjoining (d, a). In 1626 Henry Clarke yeoman of Carleton Rode left them to his son John, a baker, and John sold one shop to his brother Samuel, a haberdasher.[80] The role of the haberdashers soon seems largely to have passed to the drapers. John Craske is documented as a haberdasher in 1678 and 1682 [81] and is otherwise unrecorded, and the brief will of 1706 of Leonard Thorney haberdasher (owner of a cottage R75) directs his property to be sold to defray charges. Robert Brodewater was called haberdasher of hats at Lynn mart in 1615 [82] but chapman in 1613 when he bought the site for a marshside cottage, R9, which he subdivided in 1620 and sold in 1623. He turns up later as a tapster (a). John Fowler, feltmaker, a trade associated with hatmaking, bought a house in New Buckenham in 1695.[83] Two people made dress accessories. The pinner's wife (unnamed) was left a small legacy in 1542[84] and Stephen Griges, pointmaker, aged 30 was licensed to travel to Holland in 1630.[85] Pins were highly decorative and points were ornamental tagged laces.

A fragment of what seems to be a haberdasher's or draper's account of 1727-8 survives between the pages of a church rate book.[86] Here are mentioned green velvet, coloured herringbone, curtain, rugg, stay tapes and three sorts of buttons, solid metal, brass and 'coat buttons drabb'. The latter

---

78 See Appendix I, pp. 84-90.
79 By Wolfgang Musculus of Augsburg, prescribed reading in parish churches.
80 NRO, WAL 1090/9.
81 In will of George Woodyard, 1685, and Thomas Denny's probate inventory, 1678-9, NRO, DN/INV 60B/26.
82 NRO, KL/C 39/98.
83 Cambridge University Library, Buxton MSS 95A/60.
84 By Isabel Lister.
85 C.B. Jewson ed., *Transcript of Three Registers of Passengers from Great Yarmouth to Holland and New England 1637-1639*, NRS 25 (1954), no. 108.
86 NRO, MC 343/123.

were among 'Goods whanting for Harling'. Typically in New Buckenham with its mixed occupations the unidentified tradesman was also delivering seven bushels of malt at Kenninghall.

The location of real estate owned by New Buckenham testators beyond the town and its immediate neighbours Old Buckenham, Carleton Rode, Banham and Tibenham may roughly indicate trading links, though of course non-economic factors played a part in directing where a family held property. Ignoring very distant outliers, between 1530 and 1780 eleven wills refer to real estate between five and twelve miles north of New Buckenham, two to the north-east (and four fifteen miles away in Norwich), six to the north-west, four to the east, six to the south-east, ten to the south-west, six to the west all at nearby Wilby and Eccles, and thirty-one to the south including one at Burgate in Suffolk with outliers fourteen and fifteen miles away at Stanton and Rishangles in Suffolk. It seems that New Buckenham looked mainly to the south and south-west and to a lesser but still significant extent to the north, which are the two areas compassing the Little Ouse and Waveney Valleys and the central strip of the county north and west of Wymondham, where linen and other weavers clustered most thickly.[87] The south and south-west focus is exemplified by Thomas Jolley to whom Nesta Evans has drawn attention.[88] A linen draper from Palgrave in Suffolk whose probate inventory of 1723 lists goods at Harleston, Buckenham and Botesdale,[89] he was probably an itinerant who rented stalls at these places and stored goods in local inns and warehouses. Another Thomas Jolley did indeed hire a shop belonging to the George Inn (R74) in 1750 and 1753.[90] An earlier itinerant was Richard Russell of Tivetshall whose will of 1596 leaves two stalls in Harleston, two in Diss, and a stall with standing in Buckenham market. The New Buckenham drapers seem to have had a close and long-standing link with East Harling where by the early eighteenth century the market concentrated on linen yarn and linen cloth.[91] William Tendall in 1580, William Wade in 1664 and Stephen Gooch in 1703 all left property at Harling, Tendall's certainly and Wade's and Gooch's probably, including shops. The general trader Robert Turner also had part of his business there in 1592, John Walpole the leading New Buckenham grocer left shops there in 1736 and it was on the round of the unidentified New Buckenham haberdasher or draper of 1727-8.[92]

87 N. Evans, 'Worsted and Linen Weavers' in Ashwin and Davison, *Historical Atlas,* pp. 158-9.
88 Evans, *Rural Linen Industry,* p. 143.
89 NRO, DN/INV 75A/65.
90 NRO, DN/TER 33/1/9.
91 Evans, *Rural Linen Industry,* p. 101.
92 NRO, MC 343/123.

Leather (see Figs 5.3-4)

New Buckenham was well placed for leather production in a wood-pasture area, where oak bark for the tanpits was near at hand and where in the nearby parishes of Banham, Quidenham and East Harling chalk for the tanners' limepits could be extracted.[93] Two of the tanyards included kilns presumably for drying leather. Hides from butchering must have formed the staple of the industry, but it is possible too that deerskins came from the Knyvetts' adjacent park and the curriers and glovers evidently used dogskins. Tanning seems to have been largely self-regulating, subject to government scrutiny. Though the numbers varied a little, two searchers and one register or sealer of leather were usually appointed each year at the borough court (a). A footnote to their activities is supplied by the searchers' description in 1563 as *scrutatores corium et calcium*, inspectors of hides and shoes, that is, of the wholesale and retail sides of the business (leather was of course also used for protective and waterproof clothing generally and for such items as jerkins, belts, bottles and buckets).[94] In 1577 under pressure from a royal patentee Edward Dyer, the two searchers Robert Rysing, shoemaker, and William Colynder, currier, entered into a bond obliging them to seal only leather well wrought and sufficiently tanned.[95] That the searchers' jurisdiction was summary and did not usually result in court presentments is indicated by a note of 1628 that the lord of the borough took a third part of the value of a pair of thigh-boots or leggings (*ocrearum*) seized by the searchers (a). The retailers were the shoemakers. In 1603 and 1640 they occupied stalls formerly part of the fishmarket (a), but they evidently yielded in importance to the tanners. The 1704-5 to 1715-16 stock-in-trade ratings list no shoemakers whereas the tanners form the most important group after the drapers (f), and at this time and during most of the period under review there were always two or three tanyards in operation. They were probably not labour-intensive; the 1803 parish census records only four men engaged in tanning at a time when at least two yards, at R12 and R24, were still active.[96]

The tanyards were seen as a town asset and the borough court acted to prevent what were described as *bercelle*, barkeries, perhaps common bark stores rather than tanpits, from falling into decay. In 1580 and 1581 the inhabitants at large were fined for their non-repair, and in 1582 it was ordered that no-one should dig a sandhole (*arena*) in any ditch belonging

---

93 [J.]C. Barringer, 'Tanners and Tanning' and J. Jones and M. Manning, 'Lime Burning and Extractive Industries' in Ashwin and Davison, *Historical Atlas*, pp. 160-1, 170-1.
94 Basing, *Trades and Crafts*, pp. 85-6.
95 Bond among parish papers.
96 NRO, MC 343/123(a).

to the barkeries so that they were damaged (a). They must have been out on the common where sand digging would have occurred. The tanyards were located behind houses whose tofts backed onto the eastern and southern sections of the town moat. After the eastern arm fell out of use in the early seventeenth century the southern (King Street) ones seem to have extended backwards into the marshes beside the beck which skirted the town. This move is seen about 1627 when a small piece of marsh called Dovehouse Yard was partitioned between Nicholas Daynes and Henry Apkins, owners of tanyards at R18 and R24.[97] A meadow south of the town was called Tan Vat Meadow in 1802.[98]

Robert Carian is the first tanner recorded. A house owner in 1542 (d), by his will of 1552 he left his son John his house (R16) and marsh, the great kettle newly bound, and all his tan vats. The will of his son, John Carian, tanner, is dated 1559 and directs his wife to sell the property to bring up their children. Walter Neve (R86) gives his occupation as a tanner in 1562 (i) but appears otherwise as a prosperous yeoman. William Neve, tanner, appears briefly in 1574 when concerned in the sale of a house and stall, R57-8, not near the waters of the moat or beck. The Browne family is better documented. The first whose trade is known is John Browne, not a tanner but in the leather business as a saddler. He owned R64 from 1562 to 1565 when it included a small workshop. His thin probate inventory of 1591 gives no occupation.[99] Mathew Browne, whose house R3 lay between the market place and the town moat, made his will in 1592 and left the house and *tanfattes* to his wife Agnes for life and then to his son John. His mother was to have 'a little howse standinge by the well in my yarde' (R5, later taken into R4). His probate inventory lists hides in the lime pit, tanned *splitinges*, nineteen *tanfattes*, and bark.[100] In 1595 Agnes was ordered to cover her *kyll* with tile because of the fire risk (a). John Browne was a town trustee and tanner in 1641 (e) and he made his will as a tanner in 1658. The yard remained in operation into the next century. It was acquired in 1696 by William Wade, tanner and trustee in 1694 and rated as a tanner in 1705-6. It included *tanfattes* in 1706 (a, e, f).

John Plume's yard is unlocated. His probate inventory of 1619 reveals a flourishing business. It refers to the *kellhouse* within the tanyard, lime pits, and ten score and nine hides.[101] Evidently childless, he left his leather and personal property to William Munnings, a Bury St Edmunds' yeoman. His

97   R18, R24; British Library, Additional Charter 14577.
98   NRO, Peake & Co. 31/8/1977.
99   NRO, DN/INV 8/262.
100   NRO, DN/INV 8/245.
101   NRO, DN/INV 30/94.

wife was one of the Rose family who are recorded later as tanners.[102]

Thomas Howchin owned property in King Street from 1601 until he made his will as a tanner in 1637. His son-in-law William Pearson (probably related to Richard Pearson shoemaker, below) succeeded to part (R17), but the property is not again recorded as a tanyard until Thomas Prethero, tanner and town trustee in 1720 and 1723 (e), acquired it after 1715. The rest, R18, was sold by Howchin to Nicholas Daynes in 1627 and by Daynes in 1641 to William Baker, tanner. A relation of Baker's must be Richard Baker, yeoman, of New Buckenham but lately of Rattlesden, Suffolk. His probate inventory of 1633, besides referring to his bible and small books, mentions George Baker, tanner, and William Baker, clothier, both of Rattlesden.[103] The Bakers owned R18 until 1665. In 1680 this included a tan office when purchased by William Mower or Moore, and in 1706 it was bought by John Rose, tanner, but evidently operated by Robert Rose who is rated for stock as a tanner in 1706-7 to 1715-16 (f). John Rose's son John sold it in 1730 to Thomas Prethero. Presumably of Welsh stock–an Owen Prethero tanner occurs in 1681 (g)–Thomas by his will of 1749 left his son Owen his house with outhouses, tan office, yards and orchard in New Buckenham and property in three other parishes. Owen probably concentrated the business at R24 (below). Kinship between the Roses and Pretheros is shown by a legacy of 1727 to Hannah Rose daughter of Thomas Prethero.[104]

The other King Street tanyard was at R24. It was owned from 1601 by Henry Apkins, followed after 1627 by William Hubbard, tanner, who in 1633 leased the adjacent Brands Hill, a piece of town waste ground measuring half an acre (h), and who was a town trustee in 1641 (f). In 1655 the absentee owner conveyed R24's reversion to Thomas Green, tanner.[105] Green's son-in-law Samuel Lane *gent.* sold the property in 1688 to William Gosse butcher and a later purchaser was Thomas Richards in 1698.[106] Richards was a tanner and town trustee in 1697 (f) and he directed in his will dated 1705 that the house and tanning office were to be sold. They were bought by his father-in-law William Barber, a grazier, who in 1706 dated his own will leaving the stock of leather and other things in the tanning office to his son John (rated on stock as a tanner 1707-8 to 1713-14) and the property itself to him for six years then to another son Charles who was similarly rated in 1714- 15 to 1715-16 (f). John Barber was a tanner in 1723

102 Will of Joan Rose, 1616.
103 NRO, DN/INV 54A/95.
104 Will of Hannah Payne, 1729.
105 J.C. Tingey, 'A Calendar of Deeds enrolled within the County of Norfolk', *Norf. Arch.* 13 (1898), p. 263.
106 NRO, MC 124/1.

and 1732 (e),[107] and also a town trustee, and his son John Barber *gent.* sold the property to Owen Prethero in 1756. Owen was buried as a gentleman in 1777,[108] but R24 remained a tannery into the nineteenth century; by 1751 it had expanded over two other marshes (a). The acquisition of R24 by a butcher then a grazier shows two entrepreneurs moving into a business that used a main by-product of butchering.

A currier's business was to dress and colour leather after tanning and to cure and process lighter skins without tanning.[109] Curriers are documented intermittently and others may have doubled as glovers and used that description. William Colynder has been noted as a currier in 1577 (p. 35). Isaac Norman, who was accused in 1603 of discharging unwholesome oils into a gutter, was probably disposing of currier's waste and Robert Nunn (R15), fined in 1636 for dumping dogs' carcases in Marsh Lane, had probably removed their skins for the glove trade (a). Only two testate curriers are known. John Hadman, currier, is documented in 1652.[110] He bought the major house R62 in 1659 and by his will of 1675 he left part of the recently-subdivided property to his grandson John Jacques, including a shop 'for...his use for his trade to worke in' and also husbandry tools, the tools of his trade, and 'all my oyle'. Samuel Burroughs made his brief will as a currier in 1735.

Among the workers in finished leather were the cordwainers or shoemakers and the glovers. Robert Rysing, shoemaker, searcher of leather in 1577, has been noted (p. 35); he owned R10 and part of R62. Edmund Murton supplied shoes for paupers in 1589-90 (c). His probate inventory of 1592 lists as his main asset shoes, boots and leather valued at £6.9s.[111] For Richard Pearson shoemaker there is both a will and an inventory.[112] By the will dated 1611 his (major) house R56 was to be sold to bring up his children 'in good education' until they could be apprenticed; John Butterfeilde, shoemaker of Diss, was an executor. The house included a shop and the inventory refers to a close mucked and sown. Of comparable status was Stephen Payne, cordwainer and town trustee in 1669 (e), who in that year inherited the major house R11. His will of 1687 styles him yeoman and mentions property in five nearby parishes. Its preamble mirrors that of the woollendraper John Gooch and indicates that he was of the same Dissenting persuasion, as was his daughter Hannah. A smaller house of his,

107 Deed of 1732 among parish papers.
108 Grave slab in New Buckenham Church.
109 Swanson, *Medieval Artisans*, pp. 53-4.
110 NRO, MS 17902.
111 NRO, DN/INV 9/242.
112 NRO, DN/INV 24/124.

R64, was bought in 1678 by Charles Read, shoemaker and town trustee in 1694 (e). Benjamin Brighting, mentioned as a cordwainer in 1678,[113] was tenant of cottage property R28 in 1671 but acquired a larger house, R53, with his wife, a yeoman's widow, in 1685. The Woods lasted long. Josiah Woods, shoemaker, took a parish apprentice in 1681.[114] Town trustee in 1694 (e), he left property in New and Old Buckenham in 1723. His son Josias was tenant of a cottage, R76, in 1729 when Hannah Payne, mentioned above, left him the use of it for four years. Josias' will dated and proved in 1742 left to his son Josias property in Winfarthing and Shelfanger. Another Woods, Obediah, was a cordwainer in 1742.[115] He owned major houses R62 from 1736 and R49 from 1751 to 1755. His son William, also a cordwainer and a town trustee in 1752 (e), inherited R62 from his father in 1755 and also property in Old Buckenham and Great Ellingham. Others were Thomas Bootman who bought a cottage R31 in 1762 and made his simple will in 1775, Thomas Rush, a town trustee (e, k), who bought R19 in 1748 and in 1762 left property besides in Old Buckenham and Wilby, and John Orford who made his will in 1772 and left R60 but no property outside the town. Like shoemakers, glovers depended on a local supply of leather. John Mathew, glover, occurs in a will of 1515.[116] He is probably the man of that name, giving no occupation and naming no real estate, whose will is dated 1558. John Sharpyng, who owned R16 in 1561-80, is named as a glover in 1564-5 (c) as is Robert Webster in 1581.[117] In 1585 Webster strung the town's charter box, presumably with leather thonging (c). His brief nuncupative will is of 1598 and his house was probably R59, a small cottage. William Ostler, glover, was a deponent in the tobacco suit of 1638 (below pp. 72-3) and the Nunns were a family of glovers. There is a settlement bond dated 1625 for Robert Nunn (Robert Nunn of the dogskins) (g) and he and Henry Nunn bought a cottage, R48e, in the Bull Inn yard in 1659. In 1651 Henry agreed to take on an absconding apprentice from Gissing.[118] He made his brief will as a glover in 1675. John Nunn, glover, appears in 1746 (g). John Hayward, glover, was a town trustee in 1694 (e). His wife inherited R19 in 1684 and he sold it to his son John in 1710. Clement Palmer, glover, made his will in 1777 making Roger Foulger, glover, evidently his son-in-law, his executor. Three of the five glovers listed in the 1803 census are called Foulger.[119]

113　Probate inventory of Thomas Dennye, tailor, NRO, DN/INV 60B/26.
114　NRO, DN/BBD 81/1.
115　Deed in NRO, Taylor Vintners 6/12/1995.
116　Will of Stephen Mane, 1515.
117　When he acted as agent in the sale of R49.
118　D.E.H. James ed., *Norfolk Quarter Sessions Order Book 1650-1657*, NRS 26 (1955), pp. 9, 187.
119　NRO, MC 343/123(a).

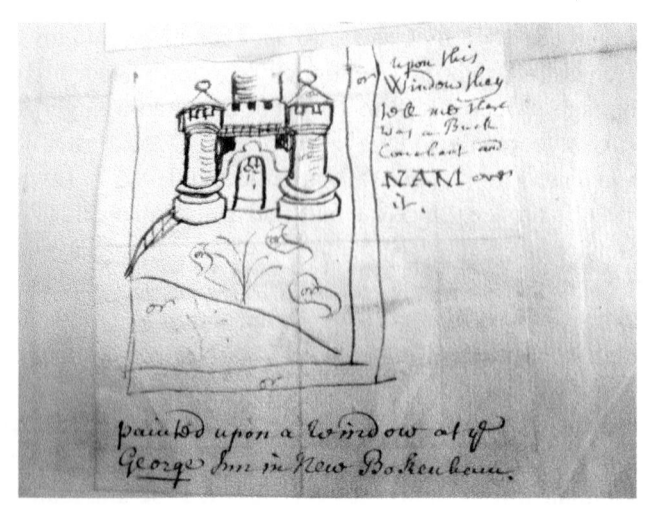

Plate 1. A drawing of glass from a window in the George Inn (R74) by Thomas Martin (1671-1771) NRO Rye 17/1. By permission of the Norfolk Record Office.

Plate 2. The obverse and reverse of a trade token issued by Francis Watts in 1657. The arms are of the Grocer's Company. The original diameter is 15 mm. From the Norfolk Token Project.

Unexpected in a semi-rural context is another worker in leather. Thomas Gibson, bookbinder of New Buckenham, who bought R28-9, then one house, in 1574, subdivided it, and sold off part in the same year. One collar (harness) maker, John Tompson, was a town trustee in 1752 (e). He owned R80.

Bread, Ale and Beer (see Figs.5.5-6)

As elsewhere, because of statutory provision, the price and quality of bread and ale were controlled at New Buckenham.[120] About 1559 the high bailiff was ordered to inspect bread offered for sale and to examine brewing vessels monthly, and the order was repeated in 1561, weighing of bread now being specified. Tasters of bread and ale were appointed at the leet court, usually two in number. Brewers, common victuallers or tapsters (*caupones*) and bakers are regularly fined at the court for breaches of the assise of bread and ale. The record survives for the years 1561-85, 1602, 1622, 1626-45 and 1650-1, with minor gaps, though all three categories do not appear in each of these years. The more elusive vintners or wine-sellers are recorded in 1582 and 1583 only. In 1562-85 brewing and baking were evidently largely part-time, domestic occupations, often carried on in the same households, though there was one detached brewhouse. For example, William Chase is fined as a brewer in 1569-71, his wife in 1574-7, and Margaret Chase widow in 1583. She is fined as a baker in 1574 and 1577-84 and as a tapster in 1582-3. It seems likely that the household brewers produced ale and the detached brewhouse the more sophisticated beer, which required hops. Brewing and baking were closely linked because of the bakers' use of yeast produced by fermenting ale.[121] In 1561-85 there were at least six brewers operating concurrently and all but two of them were also fined as bakers. The Tendalls, who owned the detached brewhouse and were therefore in a bigger way of business, did not bake, but for other households baking and brewing together must have provided a useful supplement to a variable income. An instance is Richard Mountague, brewer, vintner and baker in 1582-4 but recorded as a clerk in 1581 and a schoolmaster in 1602.[122] It is likely the womenfolk were heavily involved though it is the men who are usually named in the court records. Baking probably became more specialised in the seventeenth century; detached bakehouses begin to appear (see below) and there is also increasing competition from bakers bringing bread into the town. In 1574-84 native bakers are fined forty-four times and external and unlocated, probably not native, ones thirty-seven times. In 1626-51 the numbers are probably twenty-two and forty-eight. In contrast, because beer and ale were bulky to transport and ale did not keep or travel well,[123] only one external brewer occurs, William Burrell of Wymondham in 1629, and he must be related to the New Buckenham brewer Stephen Burrell. Of the six vintners listed in 1582-3 all but two were also brewers. In 1629-51 of the seventeen brewers fined, four are styled gentlemen, but

---

120 This paragraph comes from Source (a) unless otherwise stated.
121 J.M. Bennett, *Ale, Beer and Brewsters in England, Women's Work in a Changing World 1300-1600* (Oxford, 1996), *passim*; Swanson, *Medieval Artisans*, p. 21.
122 E.D. Stone ed., *The Lay Subsidy of 1581*, NRS 17 (1944), p. 122; will of Thomas Neve, 1603-4.
123 A. Davison, 'Malting and Brewing' in Davison and Ashwin, *Historical Atlas*, p. 164.

of the tapsters fined only one gentleman, Henry Blackett, appears (in 1641-50), and he was also a brewer. Of twelve native bakers fined in the years 1627-51 three were also brewers, one also a brewer and tapster, and one also a tapster.

It does seem from the above that native makers and sellers of beer, bread and wine were a fairly homogeneous group, though the brewers begin to emerge as the most ambitious. Some figure almost as general purveyors of foodstuffs and drink. The Chases have been mentioned, and Stephen Youngman was a brewer, baker and tapster in 1651 and in the same year was accused of selling oatmeal and butter by false measure (a). Later the Pottles combined baking and malting with innkeeping, and in the late seventeenth and the eighteenth centuries there is a tendency for grocers and medical men to move into brewing, malting and the ownership of inns. In addition, one husbandman/innkeeper, Thomas Cuttyng in 1563, and one yeoman/brewer, Henry Tendall in 1592, owned windmills.

In the notes that follow, only established inns are discussed and only one of these is identified by a name and a sign before the closing years of the sixteenth century. Other inns there must have been; Robert Geyton (R73-4), for instance, brewer and baker in 1570 and vintner in 1582-3, who in 1572 permitted gaming in his house, must have been at least the keeper of a well-established tavern (a). The oldest, and certainly as to site the largest, inn was the Bull (R47; *le bole* 1542) which dominated the entrance to the town from the direction of Norwich. Owned by Thomas Cuttyng in 1542, it was sold to John Badson by 1561. Cuttyng made his will in 1563 after the sale. Described as a husbandman, his property included a leasehold windmill at Banham and he left to the poor of New Buckenham a barrel of beer and three bushels of wheat 'to be baken in breade'. Badson was accused in 1560 of running an immoral house, harbouring suspect persons and keeping an eating and drinking house open during divine service. His bakehouse chimney was in disrepair in 1565.[124] His will, dated 1568, calls him husbandman and directs that the inn be sold. Later owners included Peter Underwood who permitted gaming in 1577 (a), Robert Gill who in 1601 bequeathed also a house in St Augustine's parish, Norwich, Osborne Stacy (will dated 1633) and the Pottles (or Pottells), Simon (will 1725), Joseph (will 1753) and Isaac (will 1762). Stacy bought another house, R25, in 1625, rebuilding it with lavish internal plasterwork.[125] In the 1634 landgable rental it is owned by his widow Elizabeth and is derisively

---

[124] NRO, ANF 1/1 and Source (a).
[125] N. Pevsner and B. Wilson, *The Buildings of England, Norfolk I: Norwich and the North-East* (1997), p. 108.

Plate 3. The market cross, reconstructed after 1716 from 16th century shops.

Plate 4. R69, the late-medieval gatehouse of the vanished mansion of the Verdon family.

Plate 5. R12, a house built c.1606 on consolidated marsh.

Plate 6. R49, an early 16th century Wealden type house.

Plate 7. R80 and R81, late 15th century houses (built on part of the market place).

Plate 8. R19 and R20, 16th and 17th century houses in King Street.

called 'pinchpot hawll' (b). Simon Pottle left the inn, now called the Black Bull, to his son Joseph. Joseph was a town trustee and baker in 1720 and trustee and innholder in 1734 (e), but he reverts to baker in his will. He left three other houses in New Buckenham as well as property in Carleton Rode and Old Buckenham. His son Isaac was styled both yeoman (k) and gentleman. His will shows that the Bull with its bowling green was sublet to Henry Scarfe (whose own simple will is dated 1762) and that he owned the New Buckenham malthouse and was a farmer besides. The Bull is last documented as an inn in 1780.[126] Gradual loss of status may be inferred by successive sales of cottage sites and one larger house plot from its curtilage between 1577 and 1660 (a). However, its offering 'Civil entertainment' to racegoers on Wilby Warren in 1722 implies it remained a place of resort.[127]

The other inns of the late sixteenth century were round the market place. The Lyon *alias* the Crown (R51) may be the inn mentioned in 1596; 'a little house adioyninge the churchyard there .... nowe is removed and standeth at the Crowne'.[128] However the will of 1595 and the inventory of the owner of the property, William Juby, husbandman, give no indication of an inn.[129] Henry Spencer who married Juby's widow was given leave in 1599 to set up the sign of the Lyon on the soil of the market place in front of the house (a). His successor was Simon Reinoulds who in the mid 1630s obtained a monopoly on the sale of tobacco at New Buckenham. The flouting of this monopoly by John Dowghty and the consequent lawsuit are mentioned below (p. 72). Reinoulds made his will in 1637 leaving the building (now certainly called the Crown) with its parlour chamber, hall chamber and green chamber, to his wife Alice for life. A silver beer bowl and a horse from the inn stable were stolen from her in 1645 (a). Later owners included Henry Mynn or Meene who bought it in 1676 and was also a maltster. Between that date and 1695 it took over the sign of the White Hart, but it had ceased trading by 1750 (a).

At the same corner of the market place was the original White Hart (R52). The building was acquired in 1599 by Richard Hulse *alias* Howes and it immediately became the centre of a celebrated dispute among the County justices, the godly faction seeking to close it as a disorderly house and the other faction backing Hulse and supported by Thomas Knyvett of Buckenham Castle, who complained of the defacement of his crest when

---

126   In a common agreement, 1780: NRO, Hastings Public Library 11/02/1966.
127   *Norwich Gazette* 27/1-3/2 and 3/2-2/3/1722.
128   NRO, PD 254/172.
129   NRO, DN/INV 12/186.

it was closed and the sign hauled down.[130] Hulse was a former servant of Sir John Fortescue the Chancellor of the Exchequer and he claimed other powerful patrons, but he was not above forgery to support his case. At all events, the inn survived. Hulse made his will in 1606 and Thomas Downes evidently married his widow. The drain from Downes' brewhouse was presented in 1609 and its defective chimney in 1612 and 1618 (a). His will of 1626 calls him yeoman and his inventory innholder[131] and they refer to a copper, brewing vessels, barley in two barns, and the long table in the long chamber. John Freeman who bought the inn in 1659 was an apothecary. It is last described as an inn in 1676 (a).

The Three Feathers (R83) which later succeeded to the sign of the Crown was built on land made available in the 1470s by the narrowing of the market place. It was a building of high status with tiled roofs, brick chimneys and carved oriel sill boards.[132] By 1634 it had been opened as an inn by Agnes Miles, a shearman's widow, and had acquired the name of the Three Feathers (b). It was renamed the Crown between the 1690s and 1718. Its owners included the Warne family, also drapers and brewers, from 1643 to after 1674; they lived at R55 and sublet the inn. By 1718 both R55 and the inn had been purchased by John Marcon, gentleman and brewer. In 1728 he sold to John Crowe, also brewer and gentleman. Crowe's widow Katherine sold the inn in 1771 and by 1780 it had been acquired by Jackson's brewery at Diss.[133] In 1783 it became the town poorhouse.[134] It was probably already in decline when Thomas Tunmore, no doubt the Crowes' tenant, was rated for the Crown in 1750 (f). His probate inventory of 1754 lists kitchen, parlour, little room and pantry with one chamber above so he probably occupied only part of the building. The little room, obviously the bar, included ten chairs and three small tables. His possessions were valued at only £36.6s.6d and £20.14s was owing to Mrs Crowe brewer and the brandy merchant.[135]

The George Inn (R74) spread over the northern part of the market place. It may have originated as an island encroachment from R51 (the Lyon/Crown). In 1542 it is described as a messuage with shops and it belonged to the Juby family (d). An enlargement of the site was permitted in 1611.

130 A. Hassell Smith, 'Justices at Work in Elizabethan Norfolk', *Norf. Arch.* 34 (1969), p. 106 and *County and Court, Government and Politics in Norfolk 1558-1603* (Oxford, 1974), pp. 106-7.
131 NRO, DN/INV 33/145.
132 NRO, BL/R 19.
133 John Crowe was brewer and town trustee 1720 and 1723 (Source e) and gentleman in his will. See also 1780 common agreement (NRO, Hastings Public Library 11/02/1966).
134 NRO, MC 343/109.
135 NRO, ANF 11/5/8.

It is first linked to liquor in 1610-14 when the drain from William Juby's brewhouse is presented as a nuisance and he is fined as a brewer from 1629 to 1640 (a). He claimed gentry status in his will of 1640 and his wife Dorothy succeeded him as a brewer (a). Her successor William Juby *gent.* in his will of 1646 mentions shops and a brewhouse with a copper and with malt, wort and guile vats,[136] and he left the property to the town if his brother's male issue failed. The bequest took effect despite legal action by the Juby family and from 1649 the George was owned and let out by the town which immediately began renovation; a pump, malt chamber and malt mill were installed (c).[137] From 1656 the brewhouse was separately hired by Stephen Gooch, brewer and charity trustee in 1669 (b, e). Three of the inn's tenants[138] were testate, John Kimin, innholder, Samuel Alderton, peruke maker, and Samuel Burroughs, currier; Alderton refers to a debt owing to Katherine Crowe the brewer. Major reconstructions are recorded in 1734 and 1814 and it was cleared away about 1870.[139] A drawing of painted glass from one of its windows is preserved.[140]

The last inn beside the market place was the King's Head (R56). It was probably an inn in 1695-6 when it went by its older name, the Broadgate (f). From 1755 to 1762 it belonged to the surgeon John Barker whose father, also a surgeon, dabbled unsuccessfully in brewing (below). By 1780 it had been renamed, no doubt in honour of the young George III, and following Barker's failure had passed to the Diss Brewery.[141] Earlier there went with the property a tavern eighty feet in length that had appeared like the George on the soil of the market place by 1542 (d). Perhaps a drinking booth rather than a developed inn, it is documented until the 1630s. The only owner known to be connected to the liquor trade was Thomas Wharton, in possession in 1561, who is fined as a brewer, baker and vintner between 1562 and 1583 (a).

The Swan (R23) in King Street may have been an inn earlier in the seventeenth century though it is not documented as such until 1676. Ownership alternated between gentlemen, who presumably sublet it, and men and women with innkeeping and brewing interests. In 1601 it was bought by Henry Wolward, referred to as a beer brewer in 1611.[142] His

---

136 Wort is an infusion of malt, and gyle is the fermenting wort.
137 NRO, MC 343/108.
138 See NRO, DN/TER 33/1.
139 NRO, MC 343/109; MC 343/110. Both the George and the King's Head appear on the picture of 1820 (Rutledge, 'New Buckenham in 1820', pp. 231-2).
140 NRO, Rye 17/1 (Plate 1).
141 1780 common agreement: NRO, Hastings Public Library 11/02/1966.
142 In Richard Pereson's will, 1611.

widow Lore brought it to Robert Norris *gent.*, town trustee in 1617 (e), from whom Christopher Sudbury acquired it and was fined as a tapster in 1624-5 (a). In 1630 Richard Kett, a Norwich merchant, sold it to Jane Segoe widow, a tapster in 1631, and in 1634 it belonged to Adam Browne, recorded as a brewer and tapster the previous year (a, b). Later gentleman owners were John Wade in 1717 and Richard Waynforth, who sold it to Thomas Kemp innholder in or shortly before 1742. Between 1711 and 1715 it changed its name to the Star (a). There seem confusingly to have been two inns on the opposite side of King Street, under the Kemp family ownership (R66-7). Christopher Kemp was rated for the Bell in 1715-16 but in 1750 the building was used as the poorhouse (f). Thomas Kemp was rated for the adjacent Rampant Horse in 1750 (f), in which year it is also referred to as the White Horse. In 1762 it was bought by the surgeon John Barker who also owned the King's Head, but he was declared bankrupt in the same year.[143] John Edwards the gentleman/linen weaver bought it in 1766. It survived as an inn, with red-painted high wooden settles, into the twentieth century.

The King's Arms (R12), well off the main thoroughfares, acquired its sign between 1713 and 1729. Owned between 1729 and 1778 by the brewing family of Crowe, it was then sold to William Gibbs, surgeon, and delicensed. In 1741 it was let by John Crowe to William Shickle, a maltster from Eye (g). In 1791 it is referred to as a former inn, 'King's Harms House' (a).

The Tendalls or Kendalls were one of the two leading yeoman families of the sixteenth century. Their prosperity came partly from brewing. They acquired R44 in 1562, a property that comprised a brewhouse in 1623 and a brewhouse and malthouse in 1680. John Tendall senior, fined as a brewer in 1562-4 (a), left by his will of 1564 his houses called the *bere houses* with the yards within itself (that is, a freestanding brewhouse; house is usually written plurally at New Buckenham at this time), with the vessels belonging, to his son Henry. The reference to *bere* reinforces the suggestion already made that it was producing beer using hops, rather than ale. That hops were grown at New Buckenham is evidenced by the *twoo hope groundes* documented in 1608 and again as the *hopp ground* in 1626. This lay immediately south-west of the town and belonged to the lord of the borough. In 1578-82 there are presentments for stealing the lord's hop poles and byelaws are passed to discourage this (a). Henry Tendall, fined as a brewer 1566-77 (a), left in 1592 the profit of his *beare howse* to his brother

---

143 NRO, MC 343/11-12.

John of Banham until his son Henry was 24. Henry inherited, and in 1623 he sold it to Stephen Burrell. Henry Blackett *gent.* followed and his brewhouse chimney was defective in 1628. His successor John Halyett *gent.* was a common brewer in 1636 and so was Giles Agas *gent.* who followed in 1640 (a). It then seems to have been divided between the Agases and the Wades (John Wade is the only brewer rated for stock in the period 1704-5 to 1715-16 (f); the Wades were also drapers) until it was acquired with the major house R55 in 1713 by John Marcon *gent.* from John Wade *gent.* Marcon was a brewer and town trustee in 1720 and 1723 (e), and had ceased trading when he made his will in 1728, though he mentions John Baggett lately his maltster. The purchaser in 1728 was John Crowe *gent.* when the property (with R55) included brewing office, malthouse, kilnhouse and shops. Crowe was a brewer and town trustee in 1730 and 1734 (e) and by his will dated 1746 he left it to his wife Katherine who carried on the business, as Samuel Alderton's will of 1750 and Tunmore's inventory of 1754[144] indicate. She sold up in 1770.

Non-household malthouses begin to appear in the seventeenth century, and it is interesting to see the town taking the initiative. In 1605-6 the town's gildhall, normally in multiple occupation at this time, included a 'maltery', and a malt chamber and malt mill were installed at the George after the town acquired it in 1649. A malthouse is also recorded at R43, next to the brewhouse already mentioned at R44. It is not described as a malthouse until 1708 but it was bought in 1639-40 by William Juby, already encountered as an innholder and brewer. Henry Meene inherited it in 1664 from his father the darnick weaver. He owned the Crown from 1676 to 1687 and made his will as a maltster in 1690. He was succeeded by his son-in-law Nicholas Yallop *gent.*, a lawyer,[145] who sold in 1715 to John Walpole and in 1720 left his wife a life-insurance policy, the onus of 'variety of business' and reckonings pending with 'severall persons'.[146] Walpole, a grocer/apothecary, left the malthouse in his own use with garden or orchard, kiln, cistern and mill to his son Horatio in 1736. It was sold to John Gibbs, grocer, in 1736. Gibbs passed it in 1760 to Isaac Pottle owner of the Bull Inn. A testate maltster is James Sturgeon whose will of 1715 records no real estate and very little personal property. He must have hired the malthouse, for which he was rated in 1715-16 (f). The probate inventories of John Wright (1727) and William Gibbs (1746) indicate a sideline in malting but they were oatmeal maker and grocer respectively.[147]

144 NRO, ANF 11/5/8.
145 NRO, NAS 1/1/20/152.
146 NRO, MC 315/16-34.
147 NRO, DN/INV 77B/30 and DN/INV 81C/77.

Bakers were generally of lower status than brewers, perhaps because baking was less capital-intensive than brewing and their equipment was simpler. Few families mainly employed in baking emerge from the breakers of assise in the late sixteenth century and separate, that is non-domestic, bread ovens do not appear before the seventeenth, and then fire risk or lack of status tends to confine them to back streets. Generally, not more than two families seem to have been principally occupied as bakers at any one time. Between 1704-5 and 1715-16 one baker was rated for stock at the lowest valuation and one at twice that amount (f). Bakers who were testate or occupied known premises include Robert Rose, a baker named in a town lawsuit in 1562 (i), who owned R63 which he passed to his son Robert in 1564. Father and son are fined as brewers and bakers in 1561-66 (a). The Murtons, Mortens or Moultons, papists in the late sixteenth century, follow.[148] Simon is fined as a baker in 1574-5 and the Widow Murton in 1576 (a). By her will of 1606 Rose Murton widow left R35 to her son Robert, fined as a baker in 1602 (a). He was succeeded by another Robert, baker and town trustee in 1627 (e), who was fined as a brewer in 1645 (a) and bought up nearby backstreet properties R34 and R36. Next come the Millers at R70-1 of whom Robert was active between 1600 and 1614 and was fined for forestalling butter and rye, John who was fined as a brewer in 1633 and for a defective bakehouse chimney the previous year, and William fined as a baker 1627-41 and with a dangerous *shudd* over his oven in 1633 (a). In 1632 Stephen Stacey baker acquired R87, a plot thirty-five feet long with an oven, split off the back end of the major house plot R86. Samuel Hyde or Ide, baker, owned R16 from 1611 to the 1650s (a, g). In 1634 John Clarke, baker and tapster 1627-51, owned R77-9, a tenement, shop and two stalls within the market place having inherited them from his father the Carleton Rode yeoman (above) (a, b). A successor was Henry Clarke ,baker, who paid poor rate 1695- 6 to 1711-12 (f). A testate baker, William Cooper, left petty legacies in 1678. Later bakers include Henry Lincoln, town trustee (e, k) and owner of R52 from 1748 to 1756, Ralph Cary a trustee in 1752 (e), and of course Joseph Pottle, baker and owner of the Bull Inn (above p. 45).

Milling

An old mill mound is shown just off the south side of the common on the 1597 map. However, depositions of 1596 state that there had been no mill on the mound within fifty years.[149] It had possibly already moved to

---

[148] T.B. Trappes-Lomax, 'Roman Catholicism in Norfolk, 1599-1780', *Norf. Arch.* 32 (1961), p. 36.

[149] NRO, MC 22/11 and PD 254/172.

its later site in the middle of the common, where it is illustrated east of the town in 1739.[150] The first recorded miller is Robert Killingworth *alias* Josse who was fined in 1571 and 1572 for taking excessive toll (a). The yeoman Henry Kendall left his young daughter Katherine his windmill 'as it stands' in 1592. John Rolfe was rated for the mill between 1695-6 and 1705-6 but he sometimes seems to have underlet between these dates (f). He was still a miller in 1721 when he took a poor girl apprentice.[151] The mill house survives. Another New Buckenham man had milling interests in a neighbouring parish. Richard Hall, owner of part R16, owned a windmill at Carleton Rode in 1649-55.[152]

Oatmeal making was carried on in one property, R46, for at least a century and it is documented in two probate inventories. The house was bought in 1576 by Godfrey Taylor, fined as a brewer in 1584 and a baker in 1577-84, but the first known connection with oatmeal is in 1602 when Daniel Taylor of Thetford, probably the son of the house not yet in possession, is presented for selling oat flour by illegal measure at New Buckenham (a). Daniel Taylor, oatmeal maker, was a town trustee in 1614 (e). He made his will as an oatmeal maker in 1632 but the probate inventory of 1633 calls him a husbandman.[153] The inventory lists in the mill house a horsemill, tubs, fans (baskets for winnowing), sieves, sacks and an old bushel; there was brewing gear in the buttery and there was an old cart. The house was sold in 1639 to Gregory Wright whose will dated 1674 calls him oatbreaker. Charles his son was a town trustee and oatmeal maker in 1694 (e). John Wright follows, whose probate inventory of 1728 shows that since 1633 the sixteenth-century house had been ceiled and subdivided to form a seven-roomed dwelling with mill house and malt office besides.[154] As well as tools, sacks &c. there were three loads of oats, eight coomb of malt, six horses, a cart, barley in the straw at Banham and out of the straw, and turnips upon the ground. The total value, £87.14s, was moderate, as was that of Daniel Taylor's inventory, £28.19s.6d, and Gregory Wright's will of 1674 gives a similar impression.

Butchers and Graziers (see Figs. 5.7-8)

Considering the size of the flesh market, native master butchers are comparatively few and there are usually only two or three operating from within New Buckenham. William Shales, butcher, is named in a town suit

150 Blomefield, *History of Norfolk* (1739-75 edn), I, opp. p. 384.
151 NRO, DN/BBD 81/1.
152 NRO, MC 1807/ 21 and 23.
153 NRO, DN/INV 40/115.
154 NRO, DN/INV 77B/30.

in 1562 (i). He conveyed R80 in 1564 but kept an interest in it until 1578. His probate inventory of 1594 lists three steers, five neat, three calves and three pigs and the contents of a well-furnished house (?R39) consisting of hall, parlour and kitchen and their chambers.[155] There were turkey and other carpets and the total value including money owed by nine New Buckenham men and one from Tibenham was £125.1s.5d. Twenty-six small trees and spars and other wood may indicate a sideline as a timber merchant. However, his prosperity is partly to be explained by the will of his son, also William, merchant and citizen and grocer of London, made in 1592 on the eve of a venture 'into the partes of beyond the seas' from which he perhaps did not return. He left his father two thirds of his personal property and he refers to the house at New Buckenham that they had bought jointly. After his parents it was to go to his brother Robert, then his apprentice, and his brother John. Robert must also have prospered. He maintained an interest in New Buckenham where between about 1600 and 1616 he sold R39, bought the major house R4-5, acquired the reversion of another, R83, from his sister Agnes Miles the shearman's widow, and speculated in other property (R20, R23, R56). Other butchers lacked such external funding. Robert Green, butcher, named with Shales in the 1562 suit, bought R30, a subdivision of a larger house, about that time. The next year he was fined for slaughtering swine in the street (a). John Youngman, active from 1566, bought a small cottage, R72 or R73, in 1569. He was probably also a grazier as in 1576 he broke byelaws by pasturing sheep on the common (a). His probate inventory of 1588 totals a modest 37s.8d.[156] Geoffrey Chambers is recorded from 1584 and the next year he is fined for putting up a post near the market well to kill meat at (a). His will dated 1605 leaves a mortgaged house (R38) and lands in Tibenham, Banham, Eccles and Old Buckenham. The Girlings owned major houses. Francis is documented from 1600 (a) and owned R82 from 1614 to about 1635. Nicholas Girling's simple will of 1618 left his wife sole legatee. Another Francis who seems to have owned R33 was fined as a tapster in 1658 (a) and bought a meadow in Banham the same year.[157] His will of 1669 calls him a butcher. The last Girling butcher, Thomas, bought R1, of which he was previously tenant, in 1692.

The Girlings had close links with the Barbers. Francis Girling's house R82 passed to John Barber after 1635, William Barber was entrusted with the disposal of Francis Girling's dwellinghouse in 1669, R33 was sold by Francis grandson of Francis Girling to John Barber in 1687, one of

---

155 NRO, DN/INV 11/34.
156 NRO, DN/INV 4/84.
157 Tingey, 'Calendar of Deeds', p. 264.

the Barbers sold a shop to Thomas Girling about 1682 (c), and R1 was previously occupied by William Barber. The only New Buckenham butchers prominent in the high bailiffs' list, the Barbers (butchers, graziers and with tanning interests, and rising into the minor gentry), were at New Buckenham for six generations between the 1630s and the 1780s. Mostly called John, their genealogy is complex. Contemporaries simplified the problem by calling one of them Spruce John Barber.[158] The first to occur is John Barber, already in business in 1632 (a), who in 1634 bought R84, a major house near the butchery. His will of 1654 shows that he was also a grazier, with sheep, lambs, heifers, cows and horses, and land at Old Buckenham. His father William bought a range of shops near the butchery in 1640 and the next year R86, a large house by the market place (a). William's other son, also William, is styled gentleman from at least 1669.[159] He inherited R86 but sold it in 1671 acquiring instead its neighbour R85. He lived to be the patriarch of the family, dying aged eighty-five in 1693 and endowing a row of almshouses within the town. His lavish will includes money legacies totalling £2,235 and refers to two shops at New Buckenham (one of them occupied by John Barber his great-nephew and principal legatee) and arranges for a funeral sermon and the distribution of eighty pairs of mourning gloves.[160] The antiquary Edward Steele has this comment on his marble-topped tomb, since lowered to floor level – 'The Defunct for whom this sumptuous Monument was erected is said to be only a Butcher'.[161] Of the sons of his brother John, John was the eldest. He acquired R85 in 1659-60 through his wife Anne Rowed and R81 on his mother's death two years later. He was butcher and town trustee in 1669 (e). R81 passed to his son John, butcher and trustee in 1675 (h), who made his will (not proved until 1688) in 1676 as a butcher leaving the house and his meadows, pastures and feedings in New and Old Buckenham to his son John after his wife's death. He also arranged that John should be apprenticed to a trade that she and 'Unckle Barber'[162] should think fitting. Both the Girlings and the Barbers employed journeymen. In a rental of 1643-4 William Barber's man and Francis Girling's man appear among stallingers hiring by the day (c). William Stagg was a young butcher in John Barber's employment but also trading on his own account, who made his will in 1688. He was setting up as a grazier as he left to members of the Barber family nine horses and twenty-five couple of ewes and lambs. To George Copping servant of

158 NRO, MC 343/11-12.
159 In Francis Girling's will, 1669.
160 NRO, MC 343/2.
161 NRO, Frere MSS, NAS 1/2/19.
162 The patriarch William Barber.

William Gosse, butcher, he left sheep and a cleaver. John the son of John Barber was gentleman and town trustee in 1694 (e) had made his will in 1711 leaving three major houses (R81, R82 and R85) in New Buckenham and land in five other parishes. There is no indication that he traded as a butcher, but in 1690 he was bailiff to Mr Harvey, owner of what remained of the Knyvetts' Old Buckenham estate. [163]

Another branch of the family sprang from the John Barber who died in 1654. His second son William was called both yeoman and gentleman.[164] He was left lands in Old Buckenham and Carleton Rode by William the patriarch who also left him £800 and forgave a £300 debt. He paid poor rate as a butcher in 1697-8 and 1698-9 (f). His own son William made his will as William Barber junior grazier in 1706 and his property lay mainly in Old Buckenham. He also had land, meadow and pasture in New Buckenham and had acquired his deceased son-in-law Thomas Richards' tannery (above). His sons were tanners not butchers. The Barbers were connected by marriage with the New Buckenham families of Rowed (grocer), Barton (glazier), Moore or Mower and Richards (tanners) and Meene (maltster). They were still in the town as farmers and minor gentry in the 1780s.[165]

As the Barbers turned away from butchering others moved in. William Gosse was active from 1688,[166] was a town trustee in 1694 and owned a market place shop in 1717-19 (e, a). He also owned R24, the tannery afterwards Thomas Richards' then William Barber's, and later the major house R66-7. John Dey was a butcher and town trustee in 1694 and yeoman and trustee in 1697, and John Davy was butcher and trustee in 1694 (e). William Coote was active between 1711 and 1752-3 and owned various properties including R69, R56 and two shops on the market place.[167] Nevil Catlyn is documented from 1759 until his death (g). He dated his will in 1789 as a yeoman. His property included R81 and R48(f), formerly the Barbers', and in 1762 he was tenant of two shops on the market place.[168] By this time the butchery had disappeared but butchers continued to trade from houses on the south side of the market place, R81 passing to John Roome Johnson butcher from Catlyn in 1772 and the back premises of R82 in 1758 to John Holland, documented as a butcher in 1760.[169]

163 B. Cozens-Hardy ed., *Norfolk Lieutenancy Journal 1676-1701,* NRS 30 (1971), p. 110.
164 Yeoman 1694 (R481) and gentleman in William Stagg's will in 1688.
165 R85, R48f, R82; will of Thomas Richards 1705; grave slab of John Barber (d. 1711) in New Buckenham church.
166 See will of William Stagg, 1688.
167 The main properties were R33 and R56. He is referred to as a butcher in 1730 in NRO, Pomeroy 18/10/1995.
168 NRO, MC 2553/1-2.
169 In will of Robert Wickes, 1760-1.

Fishmongers

Because they are not fined routinely like bakers and brewers, fishmongers are more elusive. Fish stalls are listed intermittently in the high bailiffs' accounts (c). Until the mid 1580s only one is usually recorded (though it was stated in 1566 that John Juby had erected a new stall in the fish market) (a), but between 1586 and 1682 the numbers fluctuate between three and six. However, in 1625-6 one regular stall is recorded, with further payments 'of the fish mungers in the tyme of Lent' so the additional ones probably appeared during the season that meat eating was prohibited. One trader selling bad fish came from Forncett, but the rest were apparently from New Buckenham. They included Thomas Daynes in 1597 who was also a baker and tapster; Roger Johnson in 1620 and Mary Johnson in 1624 who emptied fish water in the street; William Frier who forestalled herrings and sprats in 1620; and James Page, also a baker, who in 1617-25 threw fish water in the street, the market and the common well and regrated sprats (a). In 1629 his distraint in a market court plea was three cades of herring. A cade was a barrel holding either 600 or 750 fish. The fish stalls were still listed as an asset in 1723.[170]

Dairying

New Buckenham was in a wood-pasture area, but despite this and the emphasis on grazing and butchering, and the combined herd of ninety-eight milch cows about 1578, there are comparatively few references to dairying. This was probably largely a female concern and therefore under-recorded. The widow Batylde Tendall left her cheese press, cheese vats and milk vessels to her daughter in 1542, but as she also had an establishment at Bressingham her dairying may have been concentrated in that river-bounded parish. However, William Verdon, a wealthy yeoman, had a cheese press in his dairy in 1595, the grocer/haberdasher Robert Turner's inventory of 1592 refers to a cheesehouse, that of Robert Dey yeoman of 1588 to a cheese press, and that of William Juby, husbandman, of 1595 to a dey house or dairy.[171] Henry Hornigold, yeoman, a tenant farmer at R4, refers to his cheese chamber in his will of 1667.

Grocers and Medicine (see Fig. 5.9)

These are taken together because the occupations of grocer and apothecary (preparers and vendors of preserves as well as medicinal drugs)[172] are difficult to separate and the same men used both descriptions. As late

---

170 NRO, DN/TER 33/1/3.
171 Appendix I; NRO, DN/INV 3/79 and DN/INV 12/186.
172 U. Priestley and A. Fenner, *Shops and Shopkeepers*, p. 15.

as the mid-eighteenth century one grocer, William Gibbs, bequeathed his drugs and surgical instruments (below).

The earliest doctor known at New Buckenham is Robert Spede *ficicus* (physician) who was paid 6s.8d and a fee of 1s.8d for treating the monks of Thetford Priory in 1534-5.[173] In 1542 he owned R80, one of the houses built over the southern part of the market place (d), which by his will dated 1551 he directed to be sold, making provision for his wife's maintenance. He also owned a vacant plot east of the churchyard (? R45) and it may be conjectured that here he had his physic garden. As a literate man he was called upon to act as trustee for one New Buckenham yeoman in 1530 and to draw up a deed for another in 1542.[174]

In 1704-5 and 1715-16 there were two or three grocers operating in New Buckenham at any one time (f). As a group the value of their stock-in-trade comes next to that of the drapers and the tanners. They emerge as a separate occupation early in the seventeenth century, though Robert Turner has been noted as a haberdasher, grocer and chandler on the evidence of his probate inventory of 1592.[175] The Rowets or Rowhedes were a family of grocers. Thomas, who bought R85 in 1602, was a town trustee from 1614 (e) and made his will as a grocer in 1629. His son William was his heir but his widow was to have the chamber over the hall and the use of the oven for life. Another son, Thomas, was left £40 and reappears as a citizen and grocer of London and a New Buckenham town trustee in 1641 (e). William was a grocer and town trustee in 1627 (e), supplied the town authorities with candles in 1643-4 (c) and made his will as a grocer in 1645. His wife Elizabeth was to educate and bind out their son Thomas. The son probably did not live to inherit as the house R85 passed in 1659 to the butcher John Barber who married Ann Rowet. Francis Wattes issued a farthing token at New Buckenham in 1657 (plate 2) and is described as a grocer in 1664.[176] Judging by the will dated 1663 of his bachelor brother George, the Watts family was of the middling sort. They owned R25.

The first apothecary to find record is Henry Warner, known only from his will dated 1623. His wife was sole legatee and his only asset, goods apart, was a reversionary interest in a close at Banham. Another apothecary, John Freeman, made his will in 1675. He bought the White Hart Inn (R52) in 1659 so he was probably also an innkeeper. His estate too was modest.

173 D. Dymond ed., *The Register of Thetford Priory, part 2, 1518-1540*, NRS 60 (1995-6), pp. 630, 632.
174 Deed of 1530 among parish papers; will of Robert Cobbe, 1542.
175 Appendix I.
176 *Diss Mercury* 31/1/1986; NRO, DS 513.

Thomas Wade was a man of more substance. A town trustee and grocer in 1697 (e), he also had an interest in innkeeping since he leased the George Inn (R74) from the town in 1680 and may also have owned the Swan (R23). He bought a shop with a chamber on the market place from John Huntyng a Banham grocer in 1679.[177] He made his will in 1702 and left property, besides his New Buckenham house, in Burgh and Palgrave, Suffolk, and Banham and South Lopham. The wealthy lawyer Maurice Kendall was a kinsman. John Debenham, grocer, made his will in 1711 in his parents' lifetime. His property in New and Old Buckenham was to be sold and Thomas Blake the draper and William Gibbs, grocer, were the executors. He owned the major house R12.

Thomas Fulcher is again a man of substance. He bought a range of shops on the market place in 1684 (a), was a town trustee in 1694 and 1697, and gave his occupation indifferently as grocer and apothecary from 1692 onwards (a, f, R57-8). His grave slab of 1707 at New Buckenham calls him apothecary. He owned major houses R57-8 and R62 and his widow's will dated 1734 shows her in easy circumstances and the mother-in-law of Thomas Blake.[178] John Walpole is referred to as a gentleman in 1707-8 (f). He gives his trade as an apothecary when town trustee in 1720 and 1723 (e) and as a grocer on other occasions between 1715 and 1736 (a). Already noted as a malthouse owner, he possessed the major house R84 and he made his will in 1736. He refers to his warehouse next the market cross, two shops at East Harling, a farm at Alburgh and land in five other parishes. His stock-in-trade was to be shared between his three sons, one of whom was a Bury St Edmunds woollendraper; a daughter married the grocer William Gibbs.[179]

The Gibbses, like the Rowets, were a dynasty. William Gibbs senior is documented as a grocer from 1711,[180] and was a town trustee from 1720 (e). He bought R13, a small house on the edge of the town, in 1716 and in 1720 had acquired the major house R57 (formerly Fulcher's and since his death hired by John Walpole) which he is later said to have used as a warehouse.[181] By his will of 1744 as a grocer he left his property to his wife Mary, and to his son William 'All my Druggs and Instruments belonging to the Business of a Surgeon and Apothecary'.[182] Mary Gibbs carried on the grocery business (f). William the son, a town trustee in 1759 (k), bought R31 in 1765 and

177 Source (b); deed 1679 among parish papers.
178 Will of Sarah Fulcher, 1739.
179 Will of Mary Walpole widow, 1772 (dated 1747).
180 In John Debenham's will, 1711.
181 Deeds in private possession.
182 Proved 1748.

R12 in 1778 and died as a surgeon in 1790. He prospered enough to buy the ruins of Buckenham castle and the closes and meadows that went with them in 1786.[183] William Gibbs junior (not the son of William Gibbs senior) was rated for stock as a grocer in 1714-15 (f) and was town trustee in 1720 and 1723 (e). His will of 1744 and probate inventory of 1746[184] call him grocer and maltster and show that he was also an earthenware and glass vendor and a chandler. The inventory refers to a shop with counters and drawers, brewing house, warehouse with brandy, rum and tobacco, pot shop with 'earthing pots', white and yellow earthenware and glasses, malting office with malt mill and still, and eighty pounds of candles. He bought a tenement with two shops near the butchery in 1716 and a cottage, part of R75, in 1724 (a). By his will he directed his property to be shared between his two sons after his wife's death. His son William surrendered his share to his brother John in 1747 and set up as a weaver.[185] John owned the major house R81 from 1752 and in 1756 acquired R43, the house and malthouse formerly John Walpole's. He took over the stock of candles, gave his occupation as grocer when mortgaging in 1756 and sold up in 1761.[186] Other grocers of the mid century include Charles Crowe son of John the brewer who with Katherine his mother mortgaged R11 in 1765 and sold it in 1772 after her death,[187] Richard Clarke who owned a tenement and shops previously William and John Gibbs' from 1766 to 1773,[188] and John Willett who made his simple will in 1771.

Returning to medical men, Thomas Muddiclift is styled gentleman in Edward Warne's will of 1652 and when a town trustee in 1694 (e). His own will dated in that year calls him a physician and in 1695 after his death he is called professor (that is, practitioner) of medicine (a). He must be related to the man of the same name who was minister of New Buckenham 1675-94. In 1694 he had recently bought an estate in Old Buckenham which he left to his son James together with the books in his study, his case of instruments and his drugs. He bought R50 in 1674 and left it to his daughter Hannah. In 1696 she and her husband William Wade sold it to William Barker *gent*. The Barkers were a medical family who gained considerably by the will of a kinsman William Harnwell *gent.*, formerly of Winfarthing,[189] who had retired to New Buckenham and whose will is dated 1702. His legacies to the Barkers included leasehold houses and shops in New Buckenham, and

---

183 NRO, Hastings Public Library 11/02/1966 and his will.
184 NRO, DN/INV 81C/77. The will was proved in 1746.
185 NRO, PD 540/2.
186 NRO, Lynn Museum 13/10/1977.
187 NRO, Pomeroy 9/3/1972.
188 NRO, PD 540/2.
189 NRO, MS 18833.

£400 was to be laid out in the purchase of an estate for William Barker's youngest son John. John is referred to as a surgeon in 1703[190] and was a surgeon and town trustee 1715-1734 (e). A kinsman, Peter, was a London merchant in 1712. John extended his house site (R50) in 1706. In 1723 his estate was registered as that of a papist and it included farms at Old Buckenham, Scarning, Bressingham and Larling.[191] He is described as a beer brewer in 1729 when declared bankrupt with debts of over £2,600 and his property in the four parishes, but not the New Buckenham house, was sold. Probably in 1736, and certainly in 1737, to coincide with a race meeting, he organised assemblies at New Buckenham; and in 1739 in conjunction with an assembly he advertised public demonstrations of 'many of the philosophical experiments that were performed in Gresham College in the time of the famous Mr Boyle and ... many experiments that are now performed by the ingenious Mons. Des Aguiers' (that is, Robert Boyle, the natural philosopher, and by John Theophilus Desaguliers, inventor of the planetarium).[192] In 1731 he assigned the house at New Buckenham in trust for his young son John who acknowledged ownership in 1750. John was a town trustee (e, k) and is described as a surgeon in 1750 and 1762 and as a gentleman in 1769, and was still in practice in 1785.[193] He acquired other property in the town, and it has been seen that like his father he diversified into the liquor trade, owning the King's Head (R56) and the White Horse (R66-7) inns in the 1760s. However, like his father he was obliged to relinquish his property except for the family home when he became bankrupt in 1762.[194] His daughter Catherine boarded with the Blue Nuns in Paris from 1772 to 1777.[195]

Another medical man was Anthony Minn or Minns, surgeon and town trustee in 1723 (e), who owned R25. Less ambitious than the Barkers, his simple will is dated 1758.

Metal and Wood Workers (see Fig. 5.10-11)

Prominent in the sixteenth century, blacksmiths decline in status thereafter. Smiths were high bailiffs five times between 1550 and 1610 but

---

190 The rest of this paragraph is based mainly on deeds among the parish papers of house R50, later the New Buckenham village school.
191 NRO, C/Scb 2/2.
192 *Norwich Gazette* 28/8-4/9 1736 and 12-19/11 1739. For Boyle and Desaguliers see *Dictionary of National Biography*.
193 Overseers' accounts 1785-1810 among parish papers, under date 1785.
194 NRO, MC 343/11-12; MC 2553/1-2.
195 F. J. Devaney, *The Faithful Few, a History of Norfolk Roman Catholics 1559-1778* (Norwich, 2008), p. 50.

not later, and none became town trustees after 1614.[196] Perhaps because of the risk of spreading fire, they tended to be established in the less densely-settled parts of the town, that is to say Chapel Street and the north side of King Street, though the earliest forges recorded were on or near the market place.

John Mundes is listed in the 1542 landgable rental as holding two houses including R55 and a building called *olde forge* (R54) on the soil of the market near it (d).[197] In 1557 he sold to William Tendall, the yeoman/draper;[198] the forge later became a shop (above). William's father John, a prosperous yeoman, was presented in 1562 for having set up a forge within his messuage (R2). His will of 1563 has no reference to smithing, though R2 did later include a forge. Similarly, John Huntyng was the owner of R4, also by the market place, in 1542 (d). His will of 1557 shows him, like John Tendall, to have been an active farmer with lands in New and Old Buckenham, five servants, cows, corn 'in my berne, sollers or elles where' and poultry. He left John Edwards, his servant, half his shop gear and tools and the other half to John Huntyng, his nephew, with condition that Edwards taught the boy blacksmith's craft. The will dated 1591 of John Edwards, blacksmith, again shows farming interests with cattle, swine, and a barn recently bought from the Tendalls. His wife was left his shop with ware and implements belonging; this was on the soil of the market near R80, but his dwellinghouse, bought in 1567, was R25 (a).

In a muster roll of 1577 smiths listed are William Verby, John Youngman and Robert Megson.[199] Megson is otherwise unknown, but Verby owned R73 from 1575. By 1599 the property had passed to Robert Verby whose simple nuncupative will of 1606 calls him a locksmith. In 1597 Youngman bought R32, a very small property measuring 30 x 30 feet, that is called the *Smiths Shopp* in 1699. He was dead by 1608 but his son and grandson succeeded him and in 1647 it was bought by Simon Pottle who in the same year was given leave to extend the building by four yards (a). Simon is recorded as a blacksmith from 1637-8 to about 1660 (c),[200] and one Joseph Pottle occurs as a smith 1642-3 to 1681 (c) but does not seem to have owned the premises. Later Pottles were bakers and innkeepers.

The Payne family owned the major house R11 from 1542 onwards (d). Stephen Payne acquired it in 1562 and he and his successor of the same

196 See Tables C and D, below.
197 Rutledge, 'New Buckenham in 1542', p. 228.
198 Final Concord among parish papers.
199 P. Millican ed., *The Musters Returns ... in Norfolk 1569, 1572, 1574 and 1577 part II*, NRS 7 (1936), p. 154.
200 NRO, MC 22/9, undated.

name are recorded as blacksmiths from 1574 to 1604 and as town trustees in 1604 and 1614, though on the latter occasion called yeoman (c, e). Later in the century the then Stephen Payne became a shoemaker (above). Other more ephemeral smiths are known. Henry Blomefelde acquired the service end of R60 in 1601; in 1602 he had not repaired his smithy (a); and he sold out in 1606. William Chambers inherited R38 from his brother Geoffrey, a butcher, in 1606. He is described as a blacksmith in the will dated 1606 of Richard Hulse *alias* Howes to whom the property was mortgaged; it was sold in 1610. Humphrey Felstead's defective forge chimney is presented in 1626 and 1629. He owned R26 in 1634 but had earlier hired R66-7 where also in 1616 his forge chimney was suspect (a). Andrew Ayton or Eyton owned R30, which he seems to have rebuilt in 1618 encroaching on the town's ground. His business was apparently on the other edge of the settlement as in 1616 he occupied the smith's forge belonging to Henry Kendall (owner of R2) and in 1622-3 he was presented for erecting a shop on waste ground at the eastern end of the town (a). Benjamin Baxter who owned R31 is documented as doing smith's work for the town from 1673 to 1681 (c), but no resident house-owning smiths are known after this date.

Of other metal workers, John Howell or Howye appears as a cutler in 1565 and 1588 (a). He bought R21 in 1564 and in 1588 left his tools and shop gear to his son Thomas after his wife's death. The son is no doubt Thomas Cutteler, employed to scour the town's armour in 1592-3 (c). A later cutler is Thomas Woodes, party to a property dispute probably about 1660.[201] He owned part of the Wealden house R49 from about 1659 to 1679. John Thwayte, brazier, who owned R41 from 1696 to 1731, is documented in 1701 and rated for stock in 1704-5 to 1715-16 (h, f).

Although New Buckenham lay in an area predominately of timber-framed building down to the eighteenth century, housewrights and other woodworkers are not easy to identify. Woodman skills may have been general in the wood-pasture region or they may have been concealed under other descriptions; for instance, William Shales, a butcher, and the draper Kendalls (above) seem also to have dealt in wood in the late sixteenth and early seventeenth centuries. Thomas Underwood's will of 1528, which gives no occupation, shows him to have been a man of substance with connections with Lowestoft where he dated his will. He left 6s.8d to repair the north aisle of the church, and retained the services of a mass-priest for three years. He owned at least four houses in New Buckenham; one was R21 and another he assigned to the building of the church roof until its issues totalled nine marks (£6). He left a tenement (R10) in the back

---

201   NRO, MC 22/9.

lane to Robert Underwood 'so that he kepe it in lawfull reparacion and he to spar the tymber and take that lyeth by the repar the house and the chymneys withall, as far as it will goe stud worthe'. He owned a cowshed, a meadow, and two closes called Brokeshold (nearby in Old Buckenham, under Harling Wood). The bonds in his counter-table are mentioned and directions are given for the sale of his tools except for a belt and two wimbles. These are woodworker's tools (namely a large axe and two small gimlets) and given the telegrammic instructions as to house repair and the Lowestoft connection he was probably a housewright and possibly also a timber importer or merchant.

Thomas Golde's will of 1587 indicates he may have been a wood craftsman as he bequeathed his tools and his wood and also 'all my bookes and all my ware'. He also left frieze and leather jerkins and canvas and leather doublets, no doubt work clothes. Richard Utting, joiner and town trustee in 1648 (e), owned R1 from 1617 to 1639. After this no carpenters or joiners are encountered among the testate or property-owning class until the eighteenth century, though of course names of craftsman employed appear in the high bailiffs' and churchwardens' accounts. Two carpenters and one joiner are rated on stock-in-trade between 1704-5 and 1715-16 (f). Of these, William Colman was a multiple property owner including the major house R52. His probate inventory of 1737 indicates a seven-roomed house, with timber and a turnip cart in the yard.[202] John Ayton, carpenter, in his will of 1754, left four houses including R20, at New and Old Buckenham and land, cattle and farming implements at Banham. William Sword bought R80 in 1754 and was employed as a carpenter by the churchwardens in the 1760s and 1770s; their account of 1765-6 also includes payment for 'Beer at Swords Fire'. John Tollis, joiner, was active 1752-66,[203] and was a town trustee (k). His wife owned a tenement and two shops on the market place and he had R15 (a).

Other woodworkers and builders include one Carter who occurs as a sawyer in 1565 (a) and Austen Robinson, sawyer, documented in 1635 (g). Thomas Baldrye, sawyer, owned backstreet cottages R26 and R72 in the 1560s. Thomas Browne, mason, (that is, bricklayer), sold a recently-built cottage (R70 or R71) in 1583 and three years previously was presented for building a dangerous chimney of clay at the back of his house (a). 'Risbye the mason' built the 'George' brewhouse in 1649 using brick and pavement (floor tiles) from Wymondham. Edward Hadyson, glazier, bought R72 formerly Baldrye's in 1565. John Barton, glazier, is documented in 1630-1

202 NRO, ANF 11/3/318.
203 Churchwardens' accounts among parish papers.

(c) and he is followed by William Barton, glazier, active with his son of the same name between 1669 (e) and 1715 (f). One of them was town trustee in 1694 and 1697 (e) and they were multiple house owners (R10, R15, R28, R60). John Gall, glazier and plumber, acquired R1 from his mother in 1754, added a workshop, and sold the property the next year. He was a town trustee in 1759 (k) and was still working as a plumber in 1761.[204]

The brewing trade required coopers, and of course they supplied other hooped wooden containers besides beer barrels. These are known: Thomas Smith, hoopmaker, whose will is dated 1553 and his son John, tithingman and cooper 1569-83 (a), who owned R27 or R40; John Cooper, cooper, who made his will in 1607 and owned major houses R56 and R81 and also R61, a set of shops with chambers on the market place; William Burton, cooper, who owned part of R75 from 1675 to 1681 and leased from the town three shops converted from butchers' stalls in 1675 (h); and Henry Burton, cooper, mentioned in a will of 1736.[205] Richard Brigges was probably a cooper. He bought the Wealden house R49 in 1581 but it had previously been conveyed by William Brigges, cooper of Banham. Richard made his will as a yeoman in 1590 leaving his wife 'all my fyerwood and chippes that shall ryse of all my tymber and splentes' (laths).

Also to be counted among the woodworkers are William Keteringe, fletcher, (a tithingman in 1569-70)[206] since fletchers supplied the shafts not the ironwork of arrows,[207] and John Goddard, basketmaker. Rated for stock from 1708-9 (f), Goddard made his will in 1752. He was prosperous enough to own six houses in New Buckenham including R13, R29, R30 and R63, and he left his stock-in-trade and his working tools to Robert Chamberlain, basketmaker, evidently his partner.

Farmers and Gentlemen

The style of yeoman may or may not indicate substantial farming interests. It is difficult to evaluate since it refers to status as much as to occupation. The Reconstructions alone show a tanner (1562), a blacksmith (1566), a draper (1580), a shearman (1616), an innkeeper (1626), a tenant farmer (1667), a cordwainer (1687), a worstead weaver and a butcher (1694), all of whom described themselves on occasion as yeomen. Its implication changes over time. A man who was content with the title in the sixteenth century might in the seventeenth or eighteenth prefer the style of

---

204 NRO, MS 14420b and MC 343/11-12; deed of 1752 among parish papers.
205 Will of Elizabeth Welham, 1741.
206 Source (a).
207 H. Swanson, *Medieval Artisans*, p. 104.

gentleman and equally a tradesman might do so when he gave up business and lived on his capital, however modest that business had been. Henry Lincoln, baker and town trustee in 1759 (k), but gentleman in 1771 when he left only personalty to be shared among butcher, baker and farmer relatives, is one such. Yet the title of yeoman lingered to the end of the century as the will of 1789 of Nevil Catlyn, a yeoman but also a butcher, indicates. However, after 1600 the title of gentleman very largely supersedes it as an indication of superior status or social ambition. Only three yeomen are found, in 1614, 1697 and 1759 among the town trustees that included the elite of the borough (e). Before 1590 no resident gentleman is recorded at New Buckenham. William Verdon is called gentleman in 1590 but makes his will as a yeoman, albeit a wealthy one, in 1595.[208] After 1600 the floodgates open–heralded by Richard Hulse *alias* Howes the innkeeper of dubious reputation whom a fellow innkeeper accords the title in 1601.[209] During the rest of the century not only do the leading families of Verdon and Kendall claim gentry status but also men who can hardly be called even parish gentry; perhaps Jane Austen's term half-gentleman is apt.[210] Thirty-two individuals using the title have been noted between 1600 and 1699 of whom eight were or had been brewers or innkeepers, one a maltster, three drapers or mercers, one a physician, and two lawyers. Eight gentlemen are listed in the poor rate assessment of 1707-8 alone (f). That is not to say that as the title became less exclusive such tradesmen could not also prosper and enhance their standing. The enterprising Barbers (butchers, graziers and tanners), are a case in point in the later seventeenth century and Thomas Blake the mercer was prosperous enough to set up his son as a gentleman in the mid-eighteenth. But between 1600 and 1690 (after which the office of high bailiff rotates less and is less of a social barometer) at least seventeen gentlemen occur who are neither high bailiffs, town trustees, nor economically active members of established families. Some had probably retired to New Buckenham because of family connections or its attractions for the elderly or infirm–its compact layout, handy market, comfortable but not opulent housing and resident medical opinion. Such are Richard Sturdivant who bought R41 in 1599 and left it to his son-in-law in 1606, William Harnwell who retired to New Buckenham with considerable wealth which he distributed by his will of 1702 to his younger relations, Peter Locke who married into the armorial Keddingtons of Rushford and whose will of 1700 indicates a well-appointed house with a library of books but whose income seems to have derived solely from a lease of

208   See will of Robert Warden, 1591.
209   In will of Robert Gill, 1601.
210   Jane Austen, *Emma*, vol.2, chapter 6.

Tibenham Rectory,[211] and John Talbot whose will dated 1743 mentions only property (in Norwich). At least one county family came to ground in New Buckenham. The impoverished and suit-ridden Lovells of East Harling sold up in 1707 and John Lovell moved into the town to become the Kendalls' tenant at R2.[212] Men of status above parish gentry are notably absent, on the other hand. The only resident esquire during the whole of the seventeenth century was Charles Gostling, who in the 1630s owned R4-5, the town's largest house and the only one with extensive grounds, and who was of a Visitation family at Hickling.[213] Later owners (John Easton, a Cambridge don and Norfolk parson, and Charles Wren, cousin of Sir Christopher) were absentee[214] as were the Kendalls at R2, the neighbouring house of almost equal status, after they became esquires about the middle of the century.

Because of its small land base, and cut off as it was from much immediately convenient arable land by the castle and its demesne to the west, its own marshes and Banham common to the south, and Carleton Rode common to the east, agriculture played a relatively minor part in the economy of New Buckenham. Its residents when they wished to invest in property often did so farther afield. Of 208 testators known between 1530 and 1780 sixty-seven men and thirteen women, almost two in five, left real estate in other parishes. Beyond New Buckenham and the four adjoining parishes they can have hardly themselves farmed and the role of landlord or rentier must have been significant.

The landscape of New Buckenham has been described. The town field, Bishop's Haugh, was to the south-east, the Coole or High Field borrowed from Old Buckenham to the north, and the marshes or morrises, often tiny bits of marshland, which lay between the town and the beck that encircled it on the southern side. After 1649 the castle park measuring about eighty-six acres, immediately west of the town but in Old Buckenham parish, was broken up into closes and by 1693 it had been let to New Buckenham men.[215] Increasingly from the early years of the seventeenth century the marishes were taken as house sites or as extensions to the tanyards, but the 1634 landgable list still records four marishes, one orchard or marish, and seven orchards that were probably on the marsh (b). That apples were indeed grown there is shown by the wills of the 1550s of two tanners,

---

211   A.W.H. Clarke and A. Campling eds, *The Visitation of Norfolk A.D. 1664*, NRS 4-5 (1934), p. 262.
212   G.L. Harrison, 'A Few Notes on the Lovells of East Harling', *Norf. Arch.* 18 (1914), p. 72 and will dated 1727 of Dionisia Lovell, 1729.
213   Clarke and Campling, *Visitation*, p. 87; Cozens-Hardy and Kent, *Mayors of Norwich*, p. 81.
214   Venn, *Alumni*, 2, p. 1322 and 4, p. 470.
215   Map in NRO, Steele & Co. 23/9/1986 (*see* p. viii).

Robert Carian leaving his wife access to his marsh and half the fruit grown there and John his son describing the legacy as two bushels of apples yearly. Their house R16 included a marsh and three orchards in 1634 (b). Geese were also kept on the marshes and because of their noise or their aggression were presented as a nuisance in 1585, 1606 and 1607 (a). Two late sixteenth-century lists indicate which families held land, and presumably farmed, in the Haugh and High Fields.[216] Landowners in the Haugh in 1586 were Henry Kendall, Robert Dey, William Verdon and William Juby, and in the High Field in 1589 the New Buckenham-based owners were John Kendall, Stephen Payne, William Murton, George Dey, Thomas Neve, Robert Turner, and John Eldred *gent.* with Peter Eldred. Juby may have been an innholder, Murton was probably a baker, Turner was a grocer/haberdasher, Payne a blacksmith, and John Eldred the well-known London merchant and trader to Baghdad (below p. 69), but the rest were probably primarily landowners and farmers and they and others like them are examined in the section that follows.

The leading sixteenth-century family at New Buckenham was that of the Verdons. They were established before 1462 and by 1475 were retainers of the Knyvetts.[217] John Verdon in his will of 1491 names no children and his estate was to be expended after his wife's death in pious legacies including the repair of five local churches and the gildhall at New Buckenham. He owned six houses in the town, one of which he bequeathed as an almshouse, and land in four nearby parishes. In 1494 William Verdon left messuages in New Buckenham and Carleton Rode and land in four parishes including seven acres to be sold to sustain St Martin's gild at New Buckenham. His stepfather William Styward of Norwich and Lady Knyvett's chaplain were executors and 'myn especyall good master' Sir William Knyvett supervisor of the will. His widow Agnes remarried twice. Her wealthy last husband, William Holynshed, was of New Buckenham when he made his will in 1519 but was a landowner in Cheshire where he funded the building of a chapel at 'the Cleve of the Ege above the Holynshed'. Agnes Holynshed's will of 1523 contains numerous pious and personal legacies and gives property in New and Old Buckenham, Carleton Rode and Tibenham to her son William Verdon. The Knyvett connection was maintained as Sir Edmund Knyvett was made supervisor of the will. William describes himself in his will of 1557 as a yeoman and leaves three acres of land to his son-in-law William Neve (also of a yeoman family) and all his other lands, pastures and woods to his son William Verdon. This William Verdon's will of 1595 also calls

216   NRO, MS 4527a and Pomeroy 30/8/1995.
217   Will of Robert Verdon, 1462; R. Virgoe, 'Earlier Knyvetts', p. 261 and NRO, MS 10202.

him a yeoman but it reflects an extended lifestyle. Whereas his father left his daughters £13.6s.8d each, his own daughters get £100. Provision was made for his elder son, William, to be entered at Cambridge then at one of the Inns of Court 'to thintent to attayne to the knowledge of the lawes of this lande'. He had expanded his grandmother's and his father's estate into seven other parishes. His legacies included silver-gilt plate and table-carpets and he had adjusted his house (R56) boundaries with his neighbour, John Tendall, probably in the course of enlarging or rebuilding. The sons between whom he shared his property both assumed the style of gentleman. Jonas Verdon made his will in 1617 leaving his wife £400 beside her jointure but mentioning no real estate. His wife was an Eldred and his sisters married into the Gooches (drapers) and that of Tendall or Kendall. The family disappears from New Buckenham before 1634 (b). They are difficult to trace as house owners as they ignored the custom of registering their property before the borough court. However, they owned two houses, one with a ditch (?moated) in 1542 (d). Abuttals hint that one was on a site later subdivided as R34, R36 and R38, and the other probably covered the big corner site comprising R66-69 where the present sixteenth- and seventeenth-century houses seem to be secondary, but the fifteenth-century gatehouse survives (see Plate 4). Although in 1542 William Verdon owned the tavern on the market place and in 1595 his son possessed a brewhouse and the right to place stalls went with R56, there is little sign of commercial activity in their wills.

It was otherwise with the second family, the Kendalls or Tendalls. They came to New Buckenham from Bressingham where William Tendall (whose will was proved in 1533) held land and died. His widow Batylde made her will in 1542 at New Buckenham where her son John had settled by 1535.[218] Her well-stocked house and dairy are evident. John Tendall yeoman's will dated 1563 lists houses and land in Bressingham, Roydon, Dickleburgh, Langcroft and Langmere as well as Old and New Buckenham, and an alder-carr on Carleton Rode common. In 1542 he owned R2, a house on the east side of the market place, to which he seems to have added an adjoining tenement with shops in 1560 (d, a). His ownership of a forge and a detached brewhouse have been mentioned. The father of at least nine children, the New Buckenham property was left mainly to his son Henry. Henry also prospered. He had the highest assessment at New Buckenham in the 1581 subsidy and his will of 1592, styling him yeoman, names his son Henry as his heir and refers to a new close in the Haugh Field.[219] A daughter,

---

218   See will of William Semecroft, 1535.
219   Stone, *Lay Subsidy*, p. 122.

Katherine, was left his windmill. Henry the son owned shops near the butchery until 1603 (a) but he soon took the title of gentleman and began the move of this senior branch of the family away from New Buckenham, being of Bressingham in 1614, Winfarthing in 1617, and later of Boyland Hall.[220] However, he did not sell the brewhouse until 1624 and he retained R2, extending the site in 1627 and rebuilding the house with a stepped gable end and an impressive moulded brick entrance arch in the front wall (a, j). His son John was of Lynford Hall and mayor of Thetford and his grandson Henry a prominent lawyer, recorder of Yarmouth and husband of an heiress at North Walsham. The family continued to be buried under armorial slabs in New Buckenham church.[221]

Other yeomen who seem to have been occupied substantially in agriculture are as follows. William Semecroft in his will of 1535 refers to three houses in New Buckenham (the main one is unlocated), the big meadow called Spittlecroft there, land in the High Field, and property at Banham. He had four horses, a herd of twelve cows (six of them at service at Kenninghall) and scythes of three sizes. The corn when reaped and in the barn was to be sold. The Neves, like the Verdons and Tendalls, cover most of the century. They worked also as tanners in the 1560s and 1570s. John Newe's (*sic*) brief will is of 1510. That of 1568 of Walter Neve yeoman is more informative. He owned leasehold and freehold houses; lands, pastures and woods in Tibenham; property in Banham and Attleborough; and in New Buckenham the major house R86 with an orchard 'at morisce' (on the marsh), Spittlecroft and a meadow beside it, and closes and other land in the Haugh Field. His bequests include a silver goblet and salt and silver spoons. The will dated 1602 of Thomas Neve, yeoman, lists property in Tibenham and in Old and New Buckenham. His son Walter, yeoman and recusant in 1596,[222] sold R86 in 1618.

Robert Dey's brief will is dated 1515. His widow Isabel made her will (as Isabel Lister) in 1543 and left her house in the 'hestrete' (King Street) with its brewhouse, bakehouse and marsh, and lands in the Haugh Field, to her son John Dey. The house was sold off in 1574 (a). Her other son Robert was to have a smaller house (R39) until his son George could inherit it at eighteen. Robert is styled yeoman in his probate inventory of 1588 and when in 1581 he sold to Henry Tendall a close in the Haugh Field.[223] The inventory shows modest comfort including painted hangings to the beds

---

220 Deed of 1614 among New Buckenham parish papers; will of Miles Blithe, 1617.
221 (e); Clarke and Campling, *Visitation of Norfolk*, p. 115; W. Rye, *Norfolk Families* (Norwich, 1913), pp. 428-9; Venn, *Alumni*, 4, p. 70.
222 T.H. Bryant, *Hundred of Shropham*, p. 113.
223 NRO, MC 1030/1 and DN/INV 3/79.

and a house with hall, buttery, kitchen and bakehouse with four chambers, one of them 'where Mr Knyvett lyeth', an internal well and a handmill. Dey is also documented as a brewer and tapster (a). George Dey acknowledged possession of R39 in 1578 and had sold the house by 1606 (a).

The will of John Eldred junior, husbandman, of 1558 refers to his house and lands in New Buckenham and the expectation of property in Helmingham (*alias* Morton) on the death of his mother-in-law; his own people came from Knettishall, Suffolk. His sons Peter and John were to inherit on his wife's death and were to be 'brought up to learninge'. John Eldred (1552-1632), no doubt duly educated, prospered greatly as a London merchant, Eastern traveller, and founding director of the East India Company. He bought the manor of Great Saxham in Suffolk where he built 'Nutmeg Hall', but remained sufficiently attached to New Buckenham to endow a preaching charity there.[224] He and his brother inherited the major New Buckenham house R85, owned by their father in 1542 (d), in 1599 after their old mother's death. Their contemporaries, the Jubys, lasted into the seventeenth century. Robert Juby, yeoman, was party to a deed of 1538.[225] His will of 1542 refers generally to his tenements, meadows and pastures and his 'goods, corn and catall'. He bequeathed his 'mustardvilles' (of a mixed grey woollen cloth) gown and his marriage gown, both trimmed with black lamb, and six silver spoons. He owned R51 in 1542 (d). William Juby, yeoman, in his will of 1595 left property in New Buckenham, Bunwell and Norwich and a meadow in Carleton Rode. His probate inventory lists the contents of hall, hall chamber, kitchen, kitchen chamber, larder and dairy and refers to a mare, a cow and a bullock.[226] As mentioned above, his wife's second husband kept an inn at R51 and in the seventeenth century the Jubys embarked on brewing in their second property, the George Inn.

By his will of 1499 Thomas Barber left to his son John his house in New Buckenham and land and marshes in the High Field; a messuage and alder carr in Old Buckenham were to be sold. In 1529 Willam Barber *alias* Bannock bought from Old Buckenham Priory the new and stylish house R83 with a garden on the marsh.[227] No doubt he was related to John Banock *alias* Barber of Stradbroke, minstrel, weaver and farmer, who died in 1542.[228] His will of 1552 calls him a yeoman and gives property in New and Old Buckenham, Carleton Rode and Tibenham to his son Thomas. R83, settled on his wife Margery before their espousal, was to go to Thomas on

224 *Oxford Dictionary of National Biography;* NRO, MC 343/106.
225 NRO, MS 13959.
226 NRO, DN/INV 12/186.
227 NRO, BL/R 19.
228 N. Evans, *Rural Linen Industry,* p. 57.

her death. Thomas, then a yeoman of Tibenham, sold the house in 1568.[229] The family seems unrelated to the butcher Barbers of the seventeenth century.

In the early part of the seventeenth century two holdings begin to resolve into small farms that were eventually to share the Haugh Field between them. Charles Gostling has been mentioned as the town's only esquire. Like his neighbour, Henry Kendall, he reorganised his house site, getting leave in 1632 to extend the barn over the town moat and probably at the same time moving the house R4-5 to the centre of the curtilage, away from the market place and enclosing it with a brick wall.[230] In 1635 he listed his property which besides the house, yards, and morris or orchard comprised sixty-six acres in ten parcels behind the house in the Haugh Field. By no means all arable, three meadows (one 'wett'), one pasture close, and also two small pightles recently converted to arable were included.[231] The other farm began modestly. In 1603 Thomas Neve, already mentioned as a yeoman and farmer, sold to John Feeke a house site measuring 57 x 20 feet beside the common at the edge of the Haugh Field. By 1614 it had grown to a messuage and six acres in three closes (a). In 1770 it is described as a messuage and farm.[232] The three-celled house survives.

Of agricultural workers there is little direct record. Individual labourers and farm or other servants are mentioned by name sometimes in wills or during presentments for gaming. Few owned real estate. One day labourer, Richard Perye, made his will in 1559. He had evidently seen better times as he left a house at Rishangles in Suffolk to his daughter and her husband 'yf they cane recover it'. Francis Cann, listed as a labourer or pioneer in a muster roll of 1577,[233] seems to have owned a small inset house at R25. Another labourer, William Beale, went to sea where he died on HMS *Princesse* in 1669.[234] There is little room for commercial gardens in New Buckenham but three gardeners are known by name. John Elsden's occupation was given when he apprenticed his son in Norwich in 1611-12;[235] the aged Robert Kemp, who made his will in 1702, owned a close at Carleton Rode and a house R31 at New Buckenham; and Whittney Constable took a parish apprentice in 1733 (g).

229 Deed among New Buckenham parish papers.
230 A presentment of 1618 refers to the *tegula* of the wall – Source (a).
231 NRO, MC 343/51. A pightle was a small enclosure.
232 NRO, Pomeroy 15/9/1995.
233 P. Millican, *Musters Returns*, p. 154.
234 See his will.
235 W.M. Rising and P. Millican eds, *An Index of Norwich Apprentices, Henry VII – George II*, NRS 29 (1959), p. 60.

Services and Miscellaneous

The occasional surgeon or physician and attorney apart, professional men are few. The living was a poor one and was technically a chapelry, and the ministers were chosen and paid by the township and were not beneficed clergymen. Few were wealthy enough or stayed long enough to make wills at New Buckenham. Richard Morley made his will in 1559 and apart from evident relationship to the Dey family his interests were mainly East Dereham. Thomas Colman's will is dated 1718 and his chief concern is the benefice of Hardingham which he owned and was keeping for his son John then at Cambridge, 'I designing him to be a Clergy Man'. A young scrivener, Robert Vincent, made his nuncupative will in 1592 leaving all his goods to Thomas Fisher, except for a cow which he gave to his mother-in-law. His inventory is meagre and by its reference to stalling gear implies that he supplemented his income by market trading.[236] However, he was employed to draw up an inventory in 1588 and a will in 1589.[237] Other men of law include Thomas Shardelowe who did legal work for the town between 1639 and 1660 (c) and in 1678 simply left goods in his chamber in London to his daughter Doll and his other goods to his daughter Nancy. John Pitcher *gent.* owned R25 from 1676, was a town trustee in 1694, copied up the churchwardens' accounts, and died in 1724 aged 74.[238] Stephen Gooch (will 1690) and John Barber (will 1711) have been noted as, possibly among other things, estate bailiffs or stewards. John Lovell was a lawyer of antiquarian bent and Nicholas Yallop was probably a lawyer as well as a maltster.[239]

Two men in the 1620s were of some culture and probably of the professional class. William Smith's probate inventory of 1626 includes many (but unlisted) books, a pair of virginals, bass and treble viols, a 'citherum' (cittern), two cases of tooth picks, a watch, and two pewter chamber pots. The total, including many debts due, was nearly £358.[240] Henry Witherell's untotalled inventory of 1629 included drinking glasses, a picture, virginals, and in the shop bibles, a statute book and another book and a broken viol.[241] Neither Smith nor Witherell is known as a house owner but Smith acquired at least one piece of the Verdons' real estate.[242]

---

236 NRO, DN/INV 10/29.
237 Will of William Locke, 1589; inventory of Clement Langdon, 1588, NRO DN/INV 4/75.
238 Churchwardens' accounts 1709-51 among parish papers; grave slab in New Buckenham church.
239 NRO, NAS 1/1/11/70 and 1/1/20/152.
240 NRO, DN/INV 33/161B.
241 NRO, DN/INV 35/279.
242 NRO, DS 514.

Among the providers of services, Stephen Stacye, painter, was the owner of one small property, R75, when he made his will in 1634. The nature of his painting–no doubt it was commercial–is not evident and either he or a son of the same name is recorded as a baker (above). Nevertheless he was a man of culture with a bible and a treble violin among his household stuff. Clement Snare, barber, in his will dated 1625 left his house (R80) to his wife Anne for life but his son Thomas was to have the use of his shop with all tools and implements belonging to the trade or misterie of a barber, on condition of being 'helpfull and carefull to and for his saide mothers goode'. John Cawdwell, a barber in 1681 (g), somewhat unexpectedly owned the tannery R18 which he sold in 1706. Two perukemakers were testate. Samuel Alderton, who made his will in 1751, was also a publican, tenant of the George Inn.[243] John Poll's will is dated 1749. Evidently childless, his assets were to be shared among his relations and the only reference to his craft is to the looking-glass in the shop. Another perukemaker, Francis Perkins, gained settlement in 1760 (g). He first hired premises in or near R85, then bought a cottage behind R52 in 1770 (a). He was licensed as a phlebotomist or blood-letter in 1766.[244] Bryant Holland, perukemaker, was a town trustee in 1752 (e). He owned part of R49 and was also a baker;[245] wigs were crimped by heating in pipeclay curlers in bakers' ovens. A watchmaker, William Hawes of New Buckenham, was party to a deed in 1769 (k).

A young pipemaker from New Buckenham, Robert Parish aged 25, was licensed to emigrate to Rotterdam with his wife Elizabeth in 1637.[246] He was probably related to Thomas Parrys who from 1612 to 1638 owned a cottage inset at R25 on a plot of 41 x 21 feet. Perhaps he was emigrating to avoid literally narrow circumstances. It was tobacco that created a furore at New Buckenham just at this time. In the mid 1630s Simon Reinouldes or Reynoldes, owner of the Crown Inn, obtained a monopoly on the sale of tobacco at New Buckenham. John Dowghty, tailor, declared he would 'use a tricke to take awaye some of Reynoldes gaine' and 'sell tobacco in dispite of Reynoldes nose'. In 1638 Reynoldes brought an Exchequer suit during which witnesses deposed that Dowghty had negotiated tobacco sales at his house in the borough (that is, within the area enclosed by the town ditch) and sold beer and tobacco pipes there, but that the tobacco had actually changed hands, first in an outhouse near Buckenham Castle (in Old Buckenham parish), afterwards in a booth on New Buckenham common, and finally at a shop set up in a calf shed just outside the borough's northern

243   NRO, DN/TER/33/1/7-8.
244   NRO, DN/VSM 1/1.
245   See will of Robert Wickes, 1760/1.
246   C.B. Jewson, *Passengers from Great Yarmouth*, p. 148.

gate, again in Old Buckenham but within a quoit's cast of New Buckenham. The tobacco found buyers from Carleton Rode, Bunwell and Banham as well as New Buckenham and among the agents Dowghty used to deliver it at the northern Coole Field gate were 'little children which usually goe to scole at the howse of the sayd Doughtie'.[247]

The Poor

Because this is largely a study of traders and property owners, people with a stake in the community, the voice of the desperately poor is hardly heard. Nevertheless they existed. That poverty was a concern at New Buckenham even before the religious and social changes and inflation of the sixteenth century is shown by two wills. John Verdon left a tenement and three acres of land to the relief and comfort of the poor for evermore in 1491 and in 1494 William Verdon left seven acres to the town for the relief and comfort of the poor 'when so ever ony charge onerithe or falleth to the seid townshep'. The wording implies that poor relief was already an accepted responsibility. In 1622 the inhabitants of New Buckenham stated that whereas Old Buckenham had over 4,000 acres and about twenty poor, New Buckenham had 200 acres and about 200 poor (i). This is of course an exaggerated claim made during a lawsuit, but it does point to the special problem of a township with almost no rateable land, which at that moment was trying to retain the right to charge part of Old Buckenham to its poor rate. The borough made strenuous, if repressive, efforts through its leet court to contain the problem of poverty and vagrancy by controlling immigration into the town. Between 1559 and 1606 general orders were passed forbidding the letting of houses or rooms to poor or otherwise suspect incomers and inhabitants were fined for this offence and placed under penalty not to repeat it (a). The numbers involved cannot be calculated as whole groups are sometimes referred to, as in 1561 when Thomas Cuttyng, an innkeeper, was fined for accommmodating beggars in his house. The most usual reason given is that such persons were unable to maintain themselves and were likely to be a charge on the inhabitants at large, but others are excluded because they were of ill repute and conduct (1571), a German (*teutonicum*) (1572), an eavesdropper (1576), vagabonds (1582), and a robber (1584). General orders excluded beggars (*c.*1559) and pilferers of wood, pales and hop poles (1578). The penalties for harbouring such persons rose from 20s. in 1602 to 39s.11d in 1606. Paupers or beggars were to be let in only by leave of the high bailiff and constable (1564), the high bailiff and six other chief inhabitants (1598), and the high bailiff and

247 TNA, PRO, E 178/5534.

churchwardens (1602). The effect of the great poor laws of 1597 and 1601 was generally to transfer such responsibilities to the Justices, but there is a further exclusion order in 1623. That poverty remained acute is indicated by the legacy of £20 left by Jonas Verdon in 1617 'to sett the poore a worke to keepe them from begginge'.

Comment

This study deals mainly with the occupations of the presumed elite–office-holders, house-owners and the testate. Its conclusions are tentative. Evidence is inevitably patchy and the numbers involved are too small to provide firm data. It is not possible to tell, for example, whether a single hatter in the sixteenth century, a darnick weaver in the seventeenth, or a milliner in the eighteenth represent one-off enterprises or under-recorded but established local businesses. However, it is suggested that the town's small land base encouraged its inhabitants to turn to a range of non-agricultural livelihoods or (in many cases) combinations of livelihood. It also encouraged them to invest in property well beyond the town's bounds. New Buckenham's assets were these. The main road and the needs of the castle household brought trade to the inns and business to the market place. Borough charters ensured freehold tenure and low rentals and the town's non-parochial status meant that church dues were minimal. The town authorities acted to make the market attractive and efficient, secured freedom from toll, used the rents of borough property to relieve the inhabitants of subsidy payments, and stimulated trade by maintaining malthouses and tannery bark stores. They also sought to reduce rates by excluding beggars and poor incomers. The staple trades were cloth finishing and sale, leather production and working, butchering, brewing, baking, malting and innkeeping, and grocery and medicine. Cloth finishing (shearing and dyeing) in the sixteenth century was succeeded in the seventeenth by cloth selling, mostly woollendrapery, with subsidiary occupations such as tailoring and hosiery. Drapery declined in the eighteenth century and linen weaving became more important. Using hides from butchering and taking advantage of a good water supply, tanning was constant and with currying gave work to shoemakers, glovers and even one bookbinder. In the large fleshmarket the town butchers were supplemented by others from within a radius of seven miles. The native bakers (some of whom were also fishmongers) were joined on the market place by others from up to twelve miles distant. Baking, brewing and malting became more specialised and moved into purpose-built premises in the early seventeenth century, though there was one non-domestic beer brewery from the sixteenth. There is a windmill and one household specialises in oatmeal production for well over a century. The number of established inns as opposed to quasi-domestic taverns increases about 1600 and the early seventeenth-century innkeepers are both flamboyant and ambitious. Later, control of the inns, brewhouses and malthouses tends to pass to brewers, bakers, grocer/apothecaries and surgeons. One very enterprising grocer/haberdasher is known in the late sixteenth century but grocers and apothecaries do not fully emerge before the early seventeenth. Smiths and metalworkers are most prosperous in the sixteenth century. This is a wood-pasture settlement but woodworkers are notably absent especially in the seventeenth century, though (probably) the brewers gave employment to a plurality of coopers in the sixteenth and early seventeenth. Tables C-D indicate that drapers and mercers are prominent throughout, tanners, cordwainers and butchers gain in the mid-seventeenth century, grocers after 1600, apothecaries after 1690, and surgeons after 1720. However, it is the two leading farming families of the sixteenth century and thereafter the drapers and one clan of butchers who are probably socially the most genuinely successful and the wealthiest.

It is difficult to know how its economy fitted into a wider pattern, but both in the area from which it drew market traders and the parishes where its testators left property New Buckenham seems to look away from Norwich and its surrounding banlieu. Its links appear to be rather with the cloth-producing areas to the south and south-west and to the north.

The Knyvetts' dominance and the lack of opportunity for the expansion of holdings in a physically restricted settlement help to explain the absence of major gentry families. After 1600 the title of yeoman rapidly yields to that of gentleman, but the change is largely cosmetic and many of the gentlemen are minor indeed. Professional men–lawyers, bailiffs, surgeons, physicians–occur intermittently as do such specialists as suppliers of silk, gingerbread, tobacco and tobacco pipes, and wigs. A few, usually elderly, people of leisure are attracted in perhaps by such services, the compactness of the settlement, and the market.

Commerce is largely confined to the market place where shops, workshops, warehouses and stalls and the major houses are concentrated. The tanyards and main brew- and malthouses are functionally sited near the waters of the town moat and beck. Trades that present a fire risk such as forges and bakehouses usually keep to the back streets, though in the sixteenth century, when the smiths' status was higher, forges are found in the market area. The market declines and the market place begins to lose its primacy in the eighteenth century as the inns move to the southern part of the town, and the butchery disappears by the 1760s.

Attention should be drawn to Dissent at New Buckenham in the late seventeenth century. In 1676 forty Nonconformists are reported among an adult population of 381.[248] Wills and ecclesiastical visitation records name the leading families as the Gooches (drapers) and the Paynes (cordwainers). Three Paynes were presented for not attending church in 1677 and four Gooches in 1681[249] and John Gooch, draper, and Stephen Gooch, beerbrewer, were executors of the will of John Money, the 'Godly lecturer' of Wymondham in 1673.[250] In 1698 the Gooches belonged to the Wymondham Congregation, but New Buckenham had its own pastor, Richard Lessingham, in 1712, and a meetinghouse is recorded in 1727.[251]

New Buckenham seems to have weathered the decline of the castle household in the seventeenth century, and the number of trades recorded varies little between the sixteenth and the eighteenth centuries. The population rises between 1578 and 1676 but rises or reverts to not much more by 1803. There is no evidence of absolute long-term decline, none of relative growth, and little of physical expansion in the period 1530-1780. It seems that its assets, the enterprise of its traders and town government and the mild priviledges conferred by its borough status, were enough to offset the disadvantages arising from a very small and restricted site, and to ensure stability but little real growth.

248 Whiteman, *Compton Census*, p. 205.
249 NRO, DN/VIS 7/3 and ANF 1/11.
250 D. Ferr, 'John Money - Wymondham's Godly Lecturer', *Norf. Arch.* 47 (2007), p. 206.
251 J. Browne, *History of Congregationalism in Norfolk and Suffolk* (1877), pp. 206-7.

Table A: Occupations in New Buckenham 1500-1699

x = listed by John Pound as also found in nineteen Norfolk market towns 1500-1699
o = found in New Buckenham but not listed in the nineteen towns

	1500-99	1600-49	1650-99
apothecary		x	x
baker	x	x	x
barber		x	x
blacksmith	x	x	x
bookbinder	o		
brewer	x	x	x
butcher	x	x	x
carpenter	x	x	x
cooper	x	x	x
currier	o	o	o
cutler	x		x
draper	x	x	x
fishmonger	x	x	
fletcher	o		
gardener		x	
gingerbread-maker		o	
glazier	x	x	x
glover	x	x	x
grocer		x	x
haberdasher	x	x	x
hatter	x		
innholder/keeper	x	x	x
joiner	x	x	
linen weaver			x
locksmith		x	
maltster			o
mason	x		
mercer	x	x	x
miller	o		o
oatmeal-maker		o	o
painter		x	
physician/surgeon	x		x
pipemaker		o	
saddler	o		
sawyer	o	o	
schoolmaster		x	x
scrivener	x		
shoemaker/cordwainer	x	x	x
tailor	x	x	x
tanner	x	x	x
textile trades	x	x	x
tobacco vendor		o	
vintner	x		
weaver	x		x
worstead weaver			x
TOTALS	25x	25x	25x
	6-o	6-o	4-o

Table B: Traders coming to New Buckenham 1563-1642.

1563-1585

bakers	Wymondham 31, Moulton 5, Carleton Rode 4, Kenninghall 4, Hockham 3, Thetford 3, Wilby 2, Hingham 2, Attleborough 1
butchers	Diss 6, Kenninghall 5, Garboldisham 5, Carleton Rode 4, Fersfield 3, Dickleburgh 2, Wymondham 2
chandler	Wymondham 1
maltster	Garboldisham 1
pedder	Eccles 1

1595-1625

bacon-seller	Bunwell 1
bakers	Wymondham 4, Attleborough 3, Banham 3, Diss 2
butchers	Attleborough 4, Carleton Rode 3, Kenninghall 3, Diss 3, Old Buckenham 2, Tivetshall 2. Roydon, Moulton, Shelfanger and Ellingham one each
butter-vendors	Harling 1, Winfarthing 1
chapman	Diss 1
corn-merchant	Old Buckenham 1
maltster	Shropham 1
oatmeal-vendor	Thetford 3
woollen thread sellers	Rockland 1, Watton 1

1626-1642

bakers	Banham 16, Thetford 10, Kenninghall 5, Aslacton 2, Bunwell 1
brewer	Wymondham 1
butchers	Attleborough, Diss, Shelfanger, Hapton, Banham, one each
butter-vendor	Dickleburgh 1
(none others recorded)	

Table C: High bailiffs' occupations 1554-5 to 1689-90.

High bailiffs are named in the headings in principal sources (a), (b) and (c), in a list 1563-81 in (b), and in notes by Roger Virgoe among the parish papers. Occupations are assembled from a number of sources. In the case of multiple occupations, what seems to be the major trade is recorded. The occupations of twenty-one High Bailiffs between these dates are unknown.

Shearman ?1554-5, 1556-7, 1561-2, 1583-4, 1612-13, 1613-14	6
Blacksmith ?1554-5, 1575-6, 1589-90, 1599-1600, 1606-7	5
Tanner 1555-6, 1562-3, 1641-2, 1645-6, 1647-8, 1648-9, 1650-1, 1678-9	8

Draper/Mercer 1556-7, 1572-3, 1579-80, 1587-8, 1596-7, 1600-1, 1604-5, 1605-6, 1611-12, 1615-16, 1617-18, 1620-1, 1621-2, 1630-1, 1631-2, 1636-7, 1637-8, 1643-4, 1644-5, 1652-3, 1654-5, 1657-8, 1660-1, 1661-2, 1666-7	25
Yeoman 1558-9, 1564-5, 1567-8, 1570-1, 1571-2, 1574-5, 1576-7, 1577-8, 1582-3, 1584-5, 1586, 1588-9, 1595-6, 1598-9, 1656-7, 1676-7	16
Innkeeper 1559-60, 1622-3, 1624-5, 1635-6	4
Butcher 1569-70, 1646-7, 1651-2, 1653-4, 1662-3, 1663-4, 1665-6, 1669-70, 1670-1, 1671-2, 1679-80, 1685-6, 1686-7, 1687-8, 1688-9	15
Haberdasher/Grocer 1581-2	1
Gentleman 1597-8, 1602-3, 1603-4, 1609-10, 1610-11, 1616-17, 1623-4, 1625-6, 1627-8, 1632-3, 1633-4, 1638-9, 1683-4, 1689-90	14
Cooper 1601-2	1
Grocer 1607-8, 1614-15, 1634-5, 1639-40, 1642-3, 1664-5, 1680-1, 1681-2	8
Brewer 1608-9, 1688-9	2
Darnick Weaver 1655-6	1
Cordwainer 1658-9, 1667-8, 1674-5, 1675-6, 1677-8	5
Maltster 1668-9, 1682-3	2
Tailor 1672-3	1

Table D: Occupations Of charity trustees 1614-1759.

From principal source (c). Non-resident trustees and those without stated occupations are excluded.

OCCUPATION	1614	1627	1641	1669	1694	1697	1720	1723	1752	1759	TOTAL
Draper/Mercer	2	3	3	2	2	1	1	2	0	1	17
Grocer	1	1	0	0	1	1	2	2	0	0	8
Yeoman	1	0	0	0	0	1	0	0	0	1	3
Oatmeal-Maker	1	0	0	0	1	0	0	0	0	0	2
Gentleman/Esquire	0	1	1	3	5	2	2	1	2	2	19
Baker	0	1	0	0	0	0	1	1	2	1	6
Tanner	0	0	2	0	1	2	1	2	0	0	8
Brewer	0	0	0	1	0	0	1	1	0	1	4
Butcher	0	0	0	1	2	0	0	0	0	0	3
Cordwainer/Shoemaker	0	0	0	1	2	0	0	0	2	1	6

Glover	0	0	0	0	1	0	0	0	0	0	1
Glazier	0	0	0	0	1	1	0	0	0	1	3
Worstead-Weaver	0	0	0	0	2	0	0	0	0	0	2
Apothecary	0	0	0	0	0	1	1	1	0	0	3
Surgeon	0	0	0	0	0	0	1	2	1	2	6
Innkeeper	0	0	0	0	0	0	1	1	0	2
Peruke-Maker	0	0	0	0	0	0	0	1	0	1
Joiner	0	0	0	0	0	0	0	1	1	2
Collar-Maker	0	0	0	0	0	0	0	1	0	1
Carpenter	0	0	0	0	0	0	0	1	0	1
Linen Weaver	0	0	0	0	0	0	0	0	1	1

Table E: Assessments for stock-in-trade 1704-5 to 1715-16

From principal source (f)

Names and trades   *Assessment*

woollen drapers
Mr Richard Crowe 1704-5 to 1715-16   £87 10s
Mr Thomas Blake 1704-5 to 1715-16   £50 00s
Mr Thomas Alden 1704-5 to 1715-16   £50 00s

tanners
Mr William Wade 1704-5 to 1705-6   £37 10s
Mr John Crowe 1704-5   £37 10s
Mr Thomas Richards 1704-5 to 1705-6   £37 10s
John Barber 1707-8 to 1713-14   £37 10s
Charles Barber 1714-15 to 1715-16   £37 10s
Mr Robert Rose 1706-7 to 1715-16   £37 10s
Mr Thomas Thorne 1704-5 to 1713-14   £25 00s

grocers
Mr Thomas Sandy 1704-5 to 1707-8   £37 10s
Mr Thomas Fulcher grocer-apothecary 1704-5 to 1706-7   £37 10s
Mr John Walpole 1708-9 to 1715-16   £37 10s
John Debbenham 1710-11 to 1711-12   £37 10s
Mr William Gibbs 1704-5 to 1705-6, 1708-9 to 1715-16   £25 00s
Mr William Gibbs jun. 1714-15 to 1715-16   £12 10s

beerbrewer
Mr John Wade 1704-5   £37 10s

brazier
John Thwayte 1704-5 to 1715-16   £30 00s

bakers
Francis Richards 1704-5 to 1712-13   £25 00s
James Aldred 1713-14   £25 00s
Stephen Shortis 1714-15 to 1715-16   £25 00s
John Fenn 1704-5 to 1715-16   £12 10s

merchant tailor
Robert Stepney 1704-5 to 1706-7   £12 10s

milliner
Elizabeth Kinge 1704-5 to 1713-14   £12 10s

hosier
John Rushmer 1712-13 to 1715-16   £12 10s

carpenters
William Colman 1704-5 to 1715-16   £12 10s
Edward Gye 1714-15 to 1715-16   £12 10s

joiner
John Salmon 1704-5 to 1708-9   £12 10s

plumber and glazier
William Bar to n 1712-13 to 1714-15   £12 10s

basketmaker
John Goddard 1707-8 to 1715-16   £12 10s

no occupation
Joseph Pottle 1715-16   blank
Mrs Mary Richards 1707-8
(widow of Thomas Richards tanner)   blank

Table F: Summary of stock-in-trade list 1704-5 to 1715-16

From principal source (f)

Totals 1704-5 to 1715-16   *Mean Assessment*

Tanners	7	£37 10s
Drapers	3	£62 10s
Grocers	6	£22 05s
Bakers	4	£18 15s
Brewer	1	£37 10s

Brazier	1	£30 00s	
Carpenters	2	£12 10s	
Merchant Tailor	1	£12 10s	
Milliner	1	£12 10s	
Joiner	1	£12 10s	
Basketmaker	1	£12 10s	
Hosier	1	£12 10s	
Plumber and Glazier	1	£12 10s	

Trades found throughout 1704-5 to 1715-16

Drapers	3	Carpenters/Joiners	2
Tanners	3	Brazier	1
Grocers	3		
Bakers	2		
Brewer	1		

Table G: Stock-in-trade 1750

From principal source (f)

Name and Trade	*Rate*
Richard Curteis mercer	3s 4d
Mr Prethero tanner	3s 1½d
Mr Womac tanner	3s ½d
Mrs Mary Gibbs grocer	2s 1d
Mr John Gibbs grocer	2s 1d
Mr Lincoln baker	1s 1d
Mr Godard basketmaker	1s ½d

Table H: Trades in population listing 1803

(Norfolk Record Office MC 343/123(a))

Labourers	43	Wheelman	1
Cordwainers	13	Weaver	1
Bricklayers	10	Patten Maker	1
Shoemakers	8	Tallow Chandler	1
Farmers	7	Watchmaker	1
Carpenters	6	Worstead Weaver	1
Shopkeepers	6	Brickmaker	1
Bakers	5	Gamekeeper	1
Glovers	5	Carrier	1
Tailors	5	Excise Officer	1
Butchers	4	Currier	1
Tanners	4	Publican	1
Collarmakers	4	Cabinet Maker	1

Linen Weavers	4	Whitesmith	1
Glaziers	3	Surgeons	3
Blacksmiths	3	Coopers	3
Clerks	2	Perukemakers	2
Gentlemen	2	Schoolmasters	2
Haberdashers	2	(one with six boarders)	

Total–37 trades and professions

Also three apprentices, 17 males either described as singlemen or given no description, seven paupers in the workhouse and four widows in the almshouse. 22 households included servants. 161 men were in adult employment. Men aged between 15 and 60 totalled 150. Total population–637.

Appendix I: The Probate Inventory of Robert Turner 1592

(Norfolk Record Office DN/INV/10/414)

Capitalisation has been modernised, Roman numerals converted to Arabic ones, missing words supplied within round brackets, and the word 'price' omitted within entries. Editorial comment is in italics. The shop inventories are in two main hands and the household inventory in a third hand. A glossary follows. The house owned by Robert Turner and described in the household inventory was R57. Its upper floor was in effect an open-plan warehouse.

An inventorye of all those goodes and chatt(els) (*words lacking*) Robarde Tournas of Nue Boucckeham att the day of *(words lacking)* beyng at Est Harlyng prised & valwred by Robard Houbbard John Hawkyng Lyanye Grygges Robard Crasse Wylliam Wells Davye Peke and John Spurgeon the tente daye of Awcgust in 34th y(ear) of the rayng of owre soufferayng ladye Quen Elyzabeth

The heading is then redrafted, evidently by an official of the probate court, who names the appraisers as Robert Hubbard, John Hawkinge, Lionell Grigges, Robert Craske, William Welles and Davye Peke.

Inprimis in corsse canmus	33s.
Item in buntgynes & ossing bryges pyckelyng	20s.
Item in bocram	18s.
Item in hollands	£5
Item in boclayng	5s.
Item in dubbelettyng canmus	40s.
Item in fustchyns	£10
Item in Norryege stouff	£5
Item in syllke laesse syllke fryge and syllke bouttrennes & syllke rebbans & syllke thered	£3
Item in startwe laesse & therede	20s.
Item in taffeytte & wolle wytte	40s.
Item in chylldrynns shourtes	6s.
Item in housse and boucram	20s.
Item in lynsie wyllsie	12d.
Item in honnye salte & soepe *(and)* venyggre	£3
Item in brusses candell waxse & pacthered & papar	6s.6d.
Item in rouseng & pycke	2s.
Item in starche tryakell quycke syllvar	3s.
In crosserye	
Item grosserye	£3

APPENDICES

Item in boxsses in pottes scolles & wayettes	10s.
Item in hamparres & otylles & pacsadell	10s.
Item in horresses four	£6

Beddyng

(Item) in beddyng	40s.
(Item) wonne deske wonne cheste wonne side salldell withe the (bri)dell	10s.
Item wonne couffar & sarten naprye	5s.
Item pynes to the vallew of	3s.4d.
Item pewtar	3s.4d.
Item 3 sponnes	2d.
Item in staull gere	3s.4d.
Item wonne mortar	6s.8d.
Item in soyng hornes	1d.
Item two karpyttes	3s.4d.
Item in kolarres in pynntes & messare and all other thynges nexlyegentlye for gottenne	20s.

Sum £43.8s.7d.

The rest of the inventory seems to relate to New Buckenham rather than East Harling

Divers other goodes of the saede Robert Turners deseased prised & valewed by Robert Vincent James Fissher of Norwich Thomas Fisher Roger Thetford & John Beredge as followeth

Item 3 lb. blacke bockelles	18d.
6 oz. red waex	3d.
2 oz. of worm sed	6d.
2 oz. of sandares	2d.
5 oz. of hors sheys	15d.
½ a lb. of genger	5d.
1½ oz. of long peper	6d.
2 oz. of graynes	1d.
a lb. of not gales	8d.
7 balles of oex treckell	3d.
a lb. of red led	3d.
2 lb. treckell	12d.
a (?lb.) of oyell de baye	12d.
3 lb. norvoyll	18d.
3 lb. yellow ocker	3s.
a ston (and a) ½ of brown a spayn	21d.
46 lb. roson	3s.10d.
7 lb. starch	21d.
6 lb. preunes	12d.

6 lb. corenes	18d.
6 lb. reysenes	15d.
5 gret ston goges	15d.
a lb. of weyer	9d.
36 stone 4 lb. of tallow	£7.8s.
3 win of crosbow thred	1½d.
2 quarters of honey	16d.
a lb. of coton wecke	12d.
2 hogeshedes	2s.
3 brushes	12d.
4 lb. sope	12d.
a gret bem & skeles to it	2s.6d.
a medell bem & skeles	12d.
in ieren waytes seven ston	5s.
in ledin waytes 22 lb.	20d.
in brasen waytes a lb. & ½	12d.
a pynt pot for veneger	2d.
a shop chest in the grocerey	3s.4d.
a payer sope skolles	8d.
a aayer *(sic)* of basen skoles	6d.
a payer once skolles	3d.
ten emtey ferrkines	6d.
½ a pecke *(illegible)*neser salt	4d.
3 dobel pyntes	3d.
a gret traye for nayles	1d.
on(e) morter waieng 45 lb. & pestell 4 lb	14s.
a dosen squaer lytes	3s.8d.
on(e) gret spening whell	10d.
a quarter of sanderes	4d.
a shop chest in the lyning shop	6s.8d.
4½ bosheles of malt	5s.
14 bosheles of mestlyn	18s.8d.
½ a barell of peces	3s.4d.
a churn of bell metell *(cancelled)*	
a small talow kellere 3 gret talow kelleres	20d.
a candell skopet	2d.
a payer of pound skolles	6d.
a breasen wayte be longing to the candell ho(use)	*(lacking)*

Item one fourkine of soope	14s.
Item 8 lb. whight suger	9s.4d.
Item 12 lb. candell	3s.8d.
Item 5 oz. of sugercandie	3d.
Item a barrell of honye	£3.6s.8d.

Item 2 hewing knyves	2s.
Item two beatels	2d.
Item tried tallow 28 stonne	£5.4s.4d.
Item a bagge to trye with all	2d.
Item a candell mould	20d.
Item a candell traye	12d.
Item the steale to depe the cottones	3d.
Item one sett of spetes	2d.
Item one brasse skillet *(cancelled)*	
Item a payer of taylers sheres	2d.
Item a cutting borde	½d.

Item more, on(e) waye of whyt salt	40s.
in graye salt 6 boshales	6s.
a barell of tare	6s.8d.
1½ lb. of red seuger candey	2s.
a lb. 2 oz. of whyt candey	2s.8d.
1½ oz. of mase	12d.
6 oz. of penetes	6d.
¼ of senemen	18d.
genger 3 lb	2s.6d.
a lb. 2 oz. of peper	2s.4d.
2 lb. of graynes	2s.
1½ lb of genger	16d.
1½ lb. of anesedes	8d.
½ a lb. of raten bayn	4d.
¼ of verdegres	8d.
a lb. of quecke selver	2s.6d.
2½ lb. of be waex	20d.
¾ of terpenten	3d.
4 quer of whyt paper	9d.
3 lb. frankinsentes	12d.
1½ lb. of blacke sope	9d.
5 lb. bremston	15d.
5 lb. of bayes	16d.
a lb. leckres	3d.
1¼ lb. of blacke bokelles	8d.
20 dozen thred botenes	6d.
½ a ¼ of a thousen nayelles	6d.
8 dosen sylke botenes	12d.
a ounce of sesteres thred	12d.
2 oz. of peney sken thred	5d.
brown thred	3d.
1 payer stockines	6d.

½ a dosen blacke (?boc)kill	3d.
½ a lb. leckres	2½d.
¼ of tarmarack	2d.
½ oz. of stafes acker	1½d.
2 oz. of shomakeres heads	4d.
a dosen ½ of thembelles	3d.
a thousend maylles	3d.
30 payer of dobell coper bockelles	18d.
2 oz. of *(illegible)*elte	1(?d).
Item on(e) talow pres	2s.6d.
a talow trow	2s.6d.
a heuing knyfe & betell	12d.
8 lodes of haye	53s.4d.
a lode of straw	3s.4d.

(cancelled) wetnes to it James Fesher of Norwich Thomas Fesher & Roger Thetford John Byrredge his marke
    Summa £30.18s.11d.

More goodes of the saide decesed prised 23 Septembris anno domini 1592 by James Fisher John Birridge and Thomas Fisher as followeth viz.

In primis a cubbard in the hall with thappurtenaunces	26s.8d.
a little rownd table	4s.
the counter table	6s.8d.
a forme to it	8d.
a nother foult table	20d.
one buffitt stole	8d.
three chaires	2s.4d.
one dogg of iron a paire of tonges fyrepan three iron hakes a paire of bellowes	4s.
a candlesticke of lattin	4d.
an old silver spone	2s.6d.
two pewter candlestickes and a salt	2s.
a lattin candle sticke	6d.
fower paire of sheetes and an od one	13s.4d.
a dozen and a halfe of trenchers	8d.
two paier of old sheetes more	6s.
a nother salt	4d.
halfe a dozen of napkines a pillowbere and a towell	2s.
a chamber pot and a broken drinking pott	4d.
two brassen lawers	12d.
ten bottles of leather	8d.
a pewter pott	6d.

a brushe	4d.
37 lb. of pewter	15s.5d.

Goodes in the buttry

Two brassen ketteles	5s.
an ambry a halfe a pecke a planke and five shelves and a powdring troughe	2s.6d.
(?two) tough combes and two chest fattes	8d.
three killers two (ch)armes two boules and a cheese fate	3s.4d.
an old fan	2d.

Goodes in the palor

A posted bed and curtaines	16s.
a cubbard	6s.8d.
a truncke	12d.
stained clothes	2s.6d.
two brasspottes a kettle and a pan a chaffing dishe two paier of pottehokes	10s.6d.
an old barred chiste	12d.

Goodes belonging to the chamber

Two feather beddes three pillowes and a bowester	46s.8d.
the posted bedd with the curtians and the teaster & iron roddes and the matt and cord	30s.
a chaier of joyners worke	4s.
a nother great chaire	12d.
a coverlett of tapestry worke	20s.
a framed table and two buffitt stoles	13s.4d.
two blancketts	12d.
a square lyvery table	2s.6d.
a danske chiste	5s.
the stayned clothes with pictures and tables of gentlemenes armes	10s.
two stained curtaines	12d.

In the chamber over the hall

An old borded bedsteed	20d.
a corne skoppet and a planke and bord	4d.

In the cheeshouse

A latch pan and an old candlesticke	20d.
a cheese prese and an ambre	18d.
seaven firkines	4s.
two tubbes and a lesser tubb	2s.

In the kitching

Two dressers and a bord	14d.

Thappurtenaunces in the yeard

Faggotten and blockes	30s.
a certaine of bricke	8d.

Furniture of husbonddry

An old shod carte	6s.8d.
cart sadle stropes and cart rope	18d.
two collors three paier of traice two ring hawlters	5s.
a mucke crome	3d.

Summa £16.13s.6d.

Summa totalis huius inventarij est–£90.11s.

The inventory was exhibited on 26 February 1593

Appendix II: Glossary to Robert Turner's Inventory

Sources: J. Bristow, *The Local Historian's Glossary & Vade Mecum* (University of Nottingham, 1997 reprint); R. Milward, *A Glossary of Household, Farming and Trade Terms from Probate Inventories* (Derbyshire Record Society, 3rd edn 1986); J.H. Wilson, *Wymondham Inventories* (Centre of East Anglian Studies, Norwich, 1986 reprint); *Oxford English Dictionary* (2nd edn, 1989).

ambry, ambre, *a standing cupboard*
barred chist, *a chest banded with iron*
basen scoles, *?cup-shaped scales for weighing loose goods*
bayes, oyell de baye, *berries and oil of the sweet bay* Laurus nobilis
beatel, betell, *a wooden mallet or pounder*
bem, *the beam of a balance or steelyard*
bockelles, bokelles, *buckles*
boclayng, *bocking, woollen drugget or baize*
bocram, boucram, *buckram*
botenes, bouttrennes, *buttons*
bremston, *brimstone or sulphur*
brown a spayn, *Spanish brown, an earth used as a pigment*
buffitt stole, *buffett stool, a rectangular stool*
buntgynes, *probably buntings, bolting cloths used in sifting meal*
canmus, *canvas*
certaine, *a quantity*
chaffing dishe, *a container of burning embers on which food was kept warm*
charmes, *churns*
chest fattes, *?for cheese vats, moulds in which curd was pressed to remove the whey*
chylldrynns shourtes, *children's shirts*
corenes, *currants*
couffar, *coffer, a chest with a rounded lid*
counter table, *a table adapted for counting*
crome *see* mucke
danske chiste, *a Danish chest, no doubt of pine*
dogg, *a firedog, used to support wood on the hearth*
fan, *a shallow basket used for winnowing corn*
fate, fatte, *a vat or tub*
ferrkine, firkine, fourkine, *a barrel containing eight gallons of ale or 56 lbs. dry measure*
foult table, *a folding table*
framed table, *a joined (i.e. not trestle) table*
fryge, *fringe*
fustchyns, *fustians, coarse linen or woollen cloth*
goges *see* ston

graynes, *grains of paradise, seeds of* Amonum meleguetta, *used as a spice and in medicines*
hakes, *hooks for hanging pots from an iron bar over the fire*
heuing, hewing knyves, *knives used for chopping or slicing*
hogeshedes, *hogsheads, casks holding 48 gallons of ale*
hollands, *fine linen cloth*
horresses, *horses*
hors sheys, *probably 'horse eyes' or cowhage* (Macuna pruriens) *whose pods were used as a vermifuge*
housse, *hose, thigh-length leg coverings*
karpyttes, *carpets, at this time used as table covers*
ketteles, *open cooking pots*
killers, kelleres, kolarres, *coolers, shallow tubs for cooling milk or wort*
laesse, *lace; see* startwe *and* therede
latch pan, *dripping pan*
lattin, *an alloy resembling brass*
lawer, *a bowl, often used for hand-washing*
leckres, *licorice*
lynsie wyllsie, *linsey-wolsey, a fabric of mixed wool and flax*
lyvery table, *a side table*
mase, *the spice mace*
maylles, *probably an error for nails*
messare, *measures*
mestlyn, *maslin, mixed corn, usually wheat and rye*
mucke crome, *a hook used to unload dung*
naprye, *linen, especially table-linen*
Norryege stouff, *Norwich stuff, the new, light draperies made in Norwich*
norvoyll, *ointment for the sinews used, for example, on horses*
not gales, *nutgalls, used in making ink*
ocker, *ochre, a yellow pigment*
oex treckell, balles of, *treacle balls, presumably for giving medicine to oxen*
once skolles, *scales for weighing by the ounce*
ossing bryges pyckelyng, *coarse linen cloth or ticking, from Osnabruch in Germany*
otylles, *perhaps for French* outils, *tools or implements*
pacsadell, *pack saddle, for carrying packs or burdens*
pacthered, *pack-thread, stout thread for tying bundles or packs*
peces, *pieces, inferior quality crystallised sugar, broken sugar loaf*
pecke, *a peck, a quarter bushel or two gallons*
penetes, *pennits, burnt sugar, perhaps barley-sugar*
peney sken thred, *?thread sold at a penny a skein*
pillowbere, *pillow case*
pottehokes, *hooks, often adjustable, for hanging pots over the fire*
powdring troughe, *a salting tub for preserving meat*
pycke, *pitch*
pynes, *pins*

pyntes, pynntes, *vessels holding one pint*
raten bayn, *rat poison*
rosen, rouseng, *rosin, distillate of turpentine, derived from the gum of the pine*
salldell, *saddle*
sandares, *probably sandarac, the name given to resin of the tree* Callitris quadrivalvis, *used in the preparation of spirit varnish and pounce; to red arsinic sulphid; and to bee bread (comb containing honey)*
senemen, *cinnamon*
sesteres thred, *sister's (nun's) or fine sewing thread*
shod carte, *a cart with iron wheel rims*
shomakeres heads, *perhaps cobblers' nails*
shourtes *see* chylldrynnes
skelles, skolles, *scales*
skillet, *a small cooking-pot with tripod legs*
skopet, *a broad wooden shovel*
soyng hornes, *thimbles, apparently used in conjunction with a knife*
spetes, *spits*
squaer lytes, *presumably a kind of candle*
stafes acker, *stavesacre, an emetic and vermin poison from the seeds of the plant* Delphinium stapisagria
stained clothes, *bed or wall hangings with painted scenes or patterns*
startwe laesse, *starched lace*
steale, *a still or container, here used for dipping candles*
ston goges, *stoneware jugs*
stropes, *straps, here part of the horse harness*
taffeytte, *taffeta*
tare, *tar*
tarmaracke, *turmeric, probably for dyeing*
thembelles, *thimbles*
thered, *thread*
therede (laesse), *thread lace*
tough combes, *combs to tease out the tow from hemp or flax*
traice, *trace, part of the horse harness*
trow, *trough*
tryakell, treckell, *treacle*
waye, wey, *a variable measure of dry goods; for salt, perhaps forty bushels*
wecke, *wick*
weyer, *wire*
win, *hanks or skeins*
wolle wytte, *?white woollen cloth*
wormsed, *vermifuge, a substance to destroy intestinal worms*

Wills and Administrations referred to in the text

The text often refers to the date when the will was made. The dates given here are those of probate or of the register in which the will occurs, which may be later. Where there is a significant difference between the two, both dates are given. Where two numbers are mentioned for ANF wills, the first is the will number and the second the folio in the will register.

Alderton, Samuel	NRO, ANF wills, 1751-3, 7/239
Andrewes, William	NRO, ANF wills, 1576, Braunche f. 312
Ayton, John	NRO, ANF wills, 1754-5, 27/456
Badson, John	NRO, ANF wills, 1570, Gottes f. 98
Barber, John	NRO, ANW wills, 1653-60, f. 81 (proved 1655)
Barber, John	NRO, ANF wills, 1688, 21/327 (made 1676)
Barber, John	NRO, ANF wills, 1711, 68/183
Barber (Barbor), Thomas	NRO, NCC, 1499, Sayve f. 35
Barber *alias* Bannock, William	NRO, NCC, 1555, Beeles f. 251 (as Bannocke)
Barber, William	will dated 1692, proved ANF 1694, NRO, MC 343/2
Barber, William	NRO, ANF wills, 1706-7, 79/231
Beale, William	TNA PROB PCC wills 1669, no. 134
Blake, Thomas	NRO, NCC, 1739, Dent f. 172
Blithe (Blyth), Miles	NRO, ANF OW, 1617, no. 1
Blyth, Henry	NRO, NCC, 1711, Famm f. 579
Bootman, Thomas	NRO, ANF wills, 1775, 87/187
Brigges, Richard	NRO, ANF wills, 1594, Hardey f. 572
Briting, John	NRO, ANF wills, 1667, 130/196
Browne, John	NRO, ANF wills, 1661, f. 234
Browne, Mat(t)hew	NRO, NCC, 1591, Andrewes f. 213
Burroughs, Samuel	NRO, NCC, 1735, Suckling f. 155
Carian (Carion), John	NRO, ANF wills, 1559-60, Moundeforde f. 99
Carian (Carion), Robert	NRO, ANF wills, 1553, Bulloke f. 49
Catlyn, Nevil	NRO, ANF wills, 1797, 30/162 (made 1789)
Chambers, Geoffrey	NRO, NCC OW, 1605, no. 109
Clarke, Henry	NRO, NCC OW, 1627, no. 369
Cobbe, Robert	NRO, ANF wills, 1542, Dowsyng f. 358
Colman, Thomas	NRO, NCC, 1718, Bigot f. 121
Cooper, John	NRO, ANF wills, 1607-9. Elflett f. 142
Cooper, William	NRO, ANF wills, 1677, 106/46
Crowe, John	NRO, ANF wills, 1746-8, 71/38

Curteis, Richard	NRO, ANF admons, 1748-51, no. 194
Cuttyng (Cutting), Thomas	NRO, ANF wills, 1563-4, Waterladde f. 96
Dawes, Anne	NRO, ANF wills, 1662-3, 85/11
Debenham, John	NRO, NCC, 1711, Famm f. 607
Denny, Thomas	NRO, NCC OW, 1678, no. 35
Dey, Robert	NRO, ANF wills, 1515, Batman f. 50
Downes, Thomas	NRO, NCC, 1626, Mittings f. 223
Edwards, John	NRO, NCC, 1592, Appelyarde, f. 31
Eldred, John	NRO, ANF wills, 1558, Lyncolne f. 179
Fisher, Francis	NRO, ANF wills, 1695, 44/293
Freeman, John	NRO, ANF wills, 1680, 5/5
Fulcher, Sarah	NRO, NCC, 1739, Dent f. 179
Gibbs, William	NRO, NCC, 1746, Gostling f. 117
Gibbs, William	NRO, NCC, 1748, Abby f. 94
Gibbs, William	NRO, ANF wills, 1791, 25/161
Gill, Robert	NRO, ANF wills, 1601, Wright f. 468
Girling, Francis	NRO, ANF wills, 1669, 22/13
Girling, Nicholas	NRO, ANF OW, 1621, no. 24
Goddard, John	NRO, NCC, 1753, Smith f. 113
Golde, Thomas	NRO, ANF wills, 1588, Bockeinge f. 366
Gooch, Frances	NRO, ANF OW, 1700, no. 76
Gooch, John	NRO, ANF wills, 1680, 104/79
Gooch, Stephen	NRO, ANF wills, 1691, 48/407
Gooch, Stephen	NRO, ANF OW, 1704, no. 45
Grey, William	NRO, NCC, 1770, Sparrow f. 243
Hadman, John	NRO, ANF wills, 1675, 107/267
Hagon (Hacon), Edward	NRO, NCC, 1720, Blomfeild f. 15
Harnwell (Harmwell), William	NRO, ANF OW, 1702, no. 40
Holynshed (Holinshed), Agnes	NRO, ANF wills, 1524, Gedney f. 321
Holynshed, William	TNA, 1519, PROB 11/19/274
Hornigold, Henry	NRO, ANF wills, 1666-7, 207/136
Howchin, Thomas	NRO, ANF wills, 1640, no. 30
Howell (Howye), John	NRO, NCC, 1589, Flack f. 39
Howes (Hulste), Richard	NRO, ANF wills, 1604-6, f. 464
Huls(t)e see Howes	
Huntyng, John	NRO, NCC, 1559, Goldingham f. 24
Ince (Juce), John	NRO, ANF wills, 1684, 208/344
Juby (Joby), Robert	NRO, NCC, 1543, Cooke f. 233
Juby(e), William	NRO, NCC, 1595, Hinde f. 234
Juby, William	NRO, ANF OW, 1640, no. 105
Juby, William	NRO, NCC, 1647, Barker f. 5
Kemp(e), Robert	NRO, ANF OW, 1702, no. 62
Kendall see Tendall	
Kimin, John	NRO, NCC, 1716, Bokenham f. 212
Lincoln(e), Henry	NRO, ANF wills, 1771, 78/86

Lister, Isabel	NRO, ANF wills, 1543, Manclerke f. 16
Locke, Peter	NRO, ANF wills, 1698-9, 187/292
Locke, William	TNA, 1589, PROB 11/73/476
Lovell, Dionisia	NRO, NCC, 1729, Rudd f. 665
Mane, Stephen	NRO, ANF wills, 1515, Batman f. 103
Marcon, John	NRO, ANF wills, 1728, 62/605
Mat(t)hew, John	NRO, ANF wills, 1559, Mouneforde f. 285
Meene, Henry	NRO, ANF wills, 1690, 94/191
Meine, Robert	NRO, ANF wills, 1664, 187/62
Miles (Myles), John	NRO, ANF OW, 1615, no. 127
Miles, William	NRO, ANF wills, 1536, Gillior f. 132
Minn(s), Anthony	NRO, ANF wills, 1758-9, 182/504
Morley, Richard	NRO, NCC, 1560, Bircham f. 314
Muddiclift, Thomas	NRO, NCC, 1695, Jones f. 84
Murton, Rose	NRO, ANF wills, 1604-6, Carre f. 344
Ne(a)ve, Thomas	NRO, ANF wills, 1603-4, Offwood f. 403
Neve, Walter	NRO, ANF wills, 1568, Gottes f. 212
Newe, John	NRO, ANF wills, 1510, Sparhawk f. 79
Norman, Robert	NRO, ANF wills, 1664, 36/156
Nun(n), Henry	NRO, ANF wills, 1676, 3/335
Orford, John	NRO, NCC, 1777, Yallop f. 385
Palmer, Clement	NRO, ANF wills, 1780, 38/178
Payne (Pain), Hannah	NRO, NCC, 1729, Rudd f. 706
Payne (Paine), Stephen	NRO, ANF wills, 1689, 55/731
Pearson (Pereson), Richard	NRO, NCC, 1611, Stywarde f. 165
Perye (Perry), Richard	NRO, ANF wills, 1559, Moundeforde f. 506
Plume, John	NRO, NCC, 1619, Mason f. 96
Poll, John	NRO, ANF wills, 1751-3, 18/306
Pottles (Pottell), Isaac	NRO, ANF wills, 1762-3, 89/255
Pottles (Pottell), Joseph	NRO, ANF wills, 1751-3, 168/306
Pottle(s), Simon	NRO, ANF wills, 1724-6, 120/370
Prethero(e), Thomas	NRO, ANF wills, 1755, 149/64 (made 1749)
Reinolds (Reynolds), Simon	NRO, ANF OW, 1637, no. 16
Richards, Thomas	NRO, ANF wills, 1705, 130/118
Rose, Joan	NRO, ANF OW, 1616, no. 83
Rowet (Rowhede), Thomas	NRO, ANF OW, 1630, no. 91
Rowet(t), William	NRO, NCC, 1646, Cally f. 139
Rush, Thomas	NRO, NCC, 1770, Sparrow f. 124
Russell, Richard	NRO, NCC, 1596, Skyppon f. 170
Scarfe, Henry	NRO, ANF wills, 1769, 31/212
Semecroft, William	NRO, NCC, 1535, Godsalve f. 174
Shales, William	TNA, 1592, PROB 11/80/250
Shardelowe, Thomas	NRO, NCC OW, 1678, no. 95
Sherman, William	NRO, NCC, 1660, Tennant f. 283
Smith, Thomas	NRO, ANF wills, 1553, Bulloke f. 149

Snare, Clement	NRO, ANF wills, 1625, f. 9
Spede, Robert	NRO, ANF wills, 1551/2, Craneforth f. 269
Stacey, Stephen	NRO, ANF wills, 1634, 51/64
Stacy(e), Osborne	NRO, ANF wills, 1633, 113/31
Stagg, William	NRO, NCC OW, 1688, no. 71
Stone, Robert	NRO, ANF admons, 1763, no. 107
Sturdivant, Richard	NRO, ANF wills, 1604-6, Carre f. 399
Sturgeon, James	NRO, ANF wills, 1715-16, 122/192
Talbot, John	NRO, ANF wills, 1743-5, 78/327
Taylor, Daniel	NRO, NCC, 1634, Playford f. 21
Tendall (Tindall), Batylde	NRO, ANF wills, 1542, Dowsyng f. 328
Tendall (Kendall, Tindall), Henry	NRO, ANF wills, 1593, Hardey f. 401
Tendall, John	NRO, NCC, 1564, Marten f. 99
Tendall (Kendall), John	NRO, ANF wills, 1625, 349/90
Tendall (Tindall), William	NRO, ANF wills, 1533, Gillior f. 70
Tendall, William	NRO, ANF wills, 1580, Johnson f. 339
Thorn(e)y, Leonard	NRO, NCC, 1706, Piddocke f. 832
Underwo(o)d, Thomas	NRO, NCC, 1528, Attmere f. 57
Verby (Varby), Robert	NRO, NCC, 1607, Rowland f. 24
Verdon, John	NRO, NCC, 1501 *recte* 1491, Popy f. 74
Verdon, Jonas	TNA, 1618, PROB 11/132/566
Verdon, Robert	NRO, ANF wills, 1462, Grey f. 93
Verdon, William	NRO, ANF wills, 1494, Liber 1, f. 105
Verdon, William	NRO, NCC, 1557, Hustinges f. 261
Verdon, William	NRO, NCC, 1597, Eade f. 34
Vincent, Robert	NRO, NCC, 1592, Appleyarde f. 176
Wade, Thomas	NRO, ANF wills, 1702, no. 154
Wade, William	NRO, ANF wills, 1665, 53/12
Walpole, John	NRO, ANF wills, 1736-7, 45/285
Walpole, Mary	NRO, NCC, 1772, Crow f. 23 (made 1747)
Warden, Robert	NRO, NCC, 1591, Andrewes f. 57
Warne, Edward	TNA, 1653, PROB 11/225/465
Warner, Henry	NRO, ANF wills, 1623, no. 144
Watt(e)s, George	NRO, ANF wills, 1662-3, 100/60
Webster, Robert	NRO, ANF wills, 1598, Bradfield f. 338
Welham, Elizabeth	NRO, NCC, 1741, Jarvis f. 63
Wick(e)s, Robert	NRO, ANF wills, 1760-1, 14/11
Willett, John	NRO, ANF wills, 1777-8, 35/340 (made 1771)
Wolward (Woodward), Henry	NRO, ANF wills, 1613-14, Budd f. 139
Woods, Josiah	NRO, ANF wills, 1723, 215/198
Woods, Josias	NRO, NCC, 1742, Woodrofe f. 114
Woods, Obediah	NRO, ANF wills, 1755, 172/93
Woodyard, George	NRO, ANF wills, 1685, 76/1051
Wright, Gregory	NRO, ANF wills, 1674, 129/21
Yallop, Nicholas	NRO, NCC, 1720, Blomefeild f. 98

Principal Sources

To avoid repetition, the principal sources have been given letters. The New Buckenham parish papers referred to are now held by the NRO (PD 540 additional; ACC 2017/71). NRO stands for the Norfolk Record Office.

(a) New Buckenham borough court books c.1559-1568 (NRO, MC 1833/1) and 1561-1879 (NRO, MC 22/1-7).

(b) High bailiff's account book 1563-1686, 1747-1854 (NRO, MC 22/10). Before the 1680s these accounts are balances only. A borough terrier of 1563, a landgable rental of 1634 and a list of high bailiffs 1563-81 are included.

(c) High bailiffs' detailed annual accounts and rentals 1550-1682, with gaps, among the parish papers.

(d) Landgable rental of 1542 (NRO, MC 343/102). Printed in P. Rutledge, 'New Buckenham in 1542', *Norfolk Archaeology*, vol. 45 (2007), pp. 227-30.

(e) Town charity and town estate trust deeds recording trustees' occupations: 1614 and 1752, among the parish papers; 1627, 1641, 1697, 1720, NRO, MC 315/1-15; 1650, 1669, 1694, 1723, 1734, NRO, MC 343/106-9; 1759 see (k) below.

(f) Overseers' accounts 1695-1747 with rate lists and stock valuations 1703/4-1715/16 and 1750, among the parish papers. For the stock lists see Tables E-G.

(g) Poor law settlement, apprenticeship and bastardy papers 1612-1861 (mostly after 1680) among the parish papers.

(h) Town estate leases 1633-1701 among the parish papers.

(i) Town suit papers 1561-1622 among the parish papers.

(j) Statutory schedules of listed buildings as presented in *New Buckenham Heritage Register* issued by Breckland District Council, n.d.

(k) NRO, MC 2051/20, including a charity deed of 1759.

R Reconstructions (unpublished) recording the descent of house property within the town, based mainly on sources (a) - (d); also on deeds in NRO, principally in MC 315, MC 343, Pomeroy & Son 9/6/72, 15/11/95 and 18/10/95, and Taylor Vintners 6/12/95, on deeds in private possession in New Buckenham and on New Buckenham late Priory manor court records in NRO, PD 540/2, PT 31 and DS 491 and 514. The properties referred to are located on Fig. 4. It should be noted that there was often a time-lag between the transfer of house property and its acknowledgment before the borough court, and that the dates in the Reconstructions usually refer to the latter. A copy of the Reconstructions has been deposited in the NRO as part of ACC 2018/47.

On the whole, where the R is followed by a number (e.g. R34), this simply refers to an individual property as shown on Fig 4. Sometimes, however, it is also referring to the information known about that property as given in the Reconstructions.

Bibliography

Norf. Arch.   Norfolk Archaeology   NRS   Norfolk Record Society

Ashwin, T. and Davison, A. eds, *An Historical Atlas of Norfolk* (Chichester, 2005)
Ayers, B., 'Medieval Planned Towns' in Ashwin and Davison, *Historical Atlas* (2005)
Barringer, [J.]C., 'Norfolk Markets' and 'Tanners and Tanning' in Ashwin and Davison, *Historical Atlas* (2005)
Basing, P., *Trades and Crafts in Medieval Manuscripts*, (British Library, 1990)
Bennett, J.M., *Ale, Beer and Brewsters in England, Women's Work in a Changing World 1300-1600* (Oxford, 1996)
Beresford, M.W and St Joseph, J.K., *Medieval England, An Aerial Survey* (1979)
Blomefield, F. and others, *An Essay Towards a Topographical History of the County of Norfolk*, 1st edn 1739-75, 2nd edn 1805-10
Browne, J., *History of Congregationalism in Norfolk and Suffolk* (1877)
Bryant, T. Hugh, *The Churches of Norfolk, Hundred of Shropham*, (Norwich, 1913)
Calendar of Close Rolls 1302-7
Calendar of Patent Rolls 1566-9
Calendar of State Papers Domestic 1656-57
Clarke, A.W.H. and Campling, A. eds, *The Visitation of Norfolk A.D. 1664*, NRS 4-5 (1934)
Cozens-Hardy, B. ed., Norfolk Lieutenancy Journal 1676-1701, NRS 30 (1971)
Cozens-Hardy, B. and Kent, E.A., *The Mayors of Norwich 1403-1835* (Norwich, 1938)
Dain, A., *Assembly Rooms and Houses in Norfolk and Suffolk* (University of East Anglia M.A. Dissertation 1993)
Devaney, F.J., *The Faithful Few, a History of Norfolk Roman Catholics*

1559-1778 (Norwich, 2008)

Dunn, R.M. ed., *Norfolk Lieutenancy Journal 1660-1676*, NRS 45 (1977)

Dymond, D. ed., *The Register of Thetford Priory, part 2, 1518-1540*, NRS 60 (1995-6)

Dymond, D., 'Medieval and Later Markets' in Ashwin and Davison, *Historical Atlas* (2005)

Evans, N. *The East Anglian Rural Linen Industry: Rural Industry and Local Economy 1500-1850* (Aldershot, 1985)

Evans, N., 'Worsted and Linen Weavers' in Ashwin and Davison, *Historical Atlas* (2005)

Farr, D., 'John Money - Wymondham's Godly Lecturer', *Norf. Arch.* 47 (2007), 205-11

Harrison, G.L., 'A Few Notes on the Lovells of East Harling', *Norf. Arch.* 18 (1914), 46-77

Hassell Smith see Smith, A. Hassell

James, D.E.H. ed., *Norfolk Quarter Sessions Order Book 1650-1657*, NRS 26 (1955)

Jewson, C.B. ed., *Transcript of Three Registers of Passengers from Great Yarmouth to Holland and New England 1637-1639*, NRS 25 (1954)

Jones, J. and Manning, M., 'Lime Burning and Extractive Industries' in Ashwin and Davison, *Historical Atlas* (2005)

Kerling, N.J.M., 'Aliens in Norfolk 1436-1485', *Norf. Arch.* 33 (1963), 200-15

Longcroft, A. et al., *The Historic Buildings of New Buckenham*, Journal of the Norfolk Historic Buildings Group 2 (Norwich, 2005)

Millican, P. ed., *The Register of the Freemen of Norwich 1548-1713* (Norwich, 1934)

Millican, P. ed., *The Musters Returns...in Norfolk 1569, 1572, 1574 and 1577, part II*, NRS 7 (1936)

Pevsner, N. and Wilson, B., *The Buildings of England, Norfolk I: Norwich and the North-East* (1997)

Pound, J.F., *Tudor and Stuart Norwich* (Chichester, 1988)

Priestley, U., *The Fabric of Stuffs* (UEA, 1990)

Priestley, U. and Fenner, A., *Shops and Shopkeepers in Norwich*, (UEA, 1985)

Rising, W.M. and Millican, P. eds, *An Index of Norwich Apprentices, Henry VII-George II*, NRS 29 (1959)

Rossi, A., *New Buckenham, Norfolk, a Study of Conservation in Rural Areas* (Diploma Thesis, York University, 1973)

Rutledge, P., 'Two Borough Charters', *Norf. Arch.* 43 (1999), 313-16

Rutledge, P., 'New Buckenham in 1542', *Norf. Arch.* 45 (2007), 222-31

Rutledge, P., 'New Buckenham in 1820' in S. Ashley and A. Marsden eds, *Landscapes and Artefacts: Studies in East Anglian Archaeology presented to Andrew Rogerson* (Archeopress Archaeology, 2014)
Rye, W. ed., *Depositions taken before the Mayor and Aldermen of Norwich* (Norwich, 1905)
Rye, W., *Norfolk Families* (Norwich, 1913)
Schofield, B. ed., *The Knyvett Letters 1620-1644*, NRS 20 (1949)
Smith, A. Hassell, 'Justices at Work in Elizabethan Norfolk', *Norf. Arch.* 34 (1969), 93-110
Smith, A. Hassell, *County and Court, Government and Politics in Norfolk 1558-1603* (Oxford, 1974)
Smith, A. Hassell, 'Labourers in Late Sixteenth Century England, A Case Study from North Norfolk', *Continuity and Change* 4 (3) (1989), 367-94
Stone, E.D. ed., *The Lay Subsidy of 1581*, NRS 17 (1944)
Swanson, H., *Medieval Artisans* (Oxford, 1989)
Tingey, J.C., 'A Calendar of Deeds enrolled within the County of Norfolk', *Norf. Arch.* 13 (1898), 33-92, 125-191, 241-292
Trappes-Lomax, T.B., 'Roman Catholicism in Norfolk, 1599-1780', *Norf. Arch.* 32 (1961), 27-46
Venn, J. and J.A., *Alumni Cantabrigienses*, part 1 (Cambridge, 1922-27)
Virgoe, R., 'The Earlier Knyvetts, The Rise of a Norfolk Gentry Family, part 2', *Norf. Arch.* 41 (1992), 249-78
Whiteman, A. ed., *The Compton Census of 1676* (1986)

Index

English places are in Norfolk unless major towns or otherwise noted. (S) stands for Suffolk

Agas: family, 49; Giles, 49
ages, 83
agriculture *see* farming
Albini *see* D'Albini
Alburgh, 57
Alden, Thomas, 80
aldercarr, 67, 69
Alderton, Samuel, 47, 49, 72, 94
Aldred, James, 81
ale, 9, 41, 48; *see also* brewers and brewing
aliens, 16, 73
almshouses, 15, 53, 66, 83
ancient demesne, 15
Andrewes: Thomas, 33; William, 32, 94
Apkins, Henry, 36-7
apothecaries, 16, 24, 46, 49, 55-7, 75, 77, 80
apples, 65-6
apprentices, 27, 32, 38-9, 51-3, 70, 83
armour, town, 33, 61
arms, heraldic, 30, 45, 64, 68, 89
Aslacton, 78
assemblies, 59
Attleborough, 68, 78; market, 26
Ayton (Eyton): Andrew, 61; John, 62, 94

bacon-seller, 78
Badson, John, 42, 94
Baggett, John, 49
Baghdad, traveller to, 66
bailiff, estate, 30, 54, 71, 75
bailiffs, high, 30n; accounts, 10, 15n, 20, 31, 55, 62, 98; duties of, 41, 73; occupations of, 14, 16, 27, 32, 53, 59, 64, 78-9; sub-bailiff, 19
bakehouses, 41-2, 50, 68, 75
Baker: George, 37; Richard, 37; William, 37
bakers and baking, 16, 25-6, 33, 41-3, 45, 47, 50-1, 60, 64, 66, 72, 74-5, 77-9, 81-2; regulation of, 26, 41; *see also* bread ovens
Baldrye, Thomas, 62
Banham, 34, 49, 51-2, 56-7, 62-3, 68, 73,
78; chalk from, 35; common, 65; windmill, 42
bankruptcy, 48, 59
Bannock *see* Barber
Barber *alias* Bannock: John, 60; Margery, 69; Thomas, 69-70; William, 69, 94
Barber: Charles, 37, 80; family, 31, 53-4, 64, 70; John, 31, 37-8, 52-4, 69, 71, 80, 94; Thomas, 69, 94; William, 15n, 37, 52-4, 94
barbers, 72, 77
bark stores/barkeries, 35-6, 74
Barker: Catherine, 59; family, 58; John, 47-8, 59; Peter, 59; William, 58-9
Barton: family, 54; John, 62; William, 63, 81
basket maker, 63, 81-2
Baxter, Benjamin, 61
Beale, William, 70, 94
bedding, 85, 88-9
beer, 41-2, 45, 48, 72; *see also* brewers and brewing
beggars, 73-4
Beredge (Birridge, Byrredge), John, 85, 88
Bickley, Sir Francis, 30
Blackett, Henry, 42, 49
blacksmiths, 16, 24-5, 59-61, 63, 66, 75, 77-8, 83; *see also* forges
Blake: Fulcher, 31; Thomas, 31, 57, 64, 80, 94
Blithe (Blyth): Henry, 27, 94; Miles, 68n, 94
Blomefelde, Henry, 61
bookbinder, 40, 74, 77
books, 29, 33, 37, 58, 62, 71-2; library, 64
Bootman, Thomas, 39, 94
borough charters *see* Buckenham, New
Botesdale (S), 34
bowling green, 45
Boyland Hall, 68
Boyle, Robert, experiments of, 59
brandy, 46, 58
braziers, 16, 61, 81-2
bread ovens, 50
Bressingham, 55, 59, 67-8
brewers and brewing, 15-16, 25, 41-2, 46-51, 58-9, 64, 69, 74-7, 79-82; equipment, 46-7; regulation of, 26, 41
brewhouses, 22, 41, 46-9, 62, 67-8, 75
brick and tile, 34, 40, 62, 90
bricklayer *see* masons
brickmaker, 82

102

INDEX

Brigges: Richard, 63, 94; William, 63
Briting (Brighting): Benjamin, 39; John, 27, 94
Brodewater, Robert, 33
Brown(e): Adam, 48; Agnes, 36; John, 36, 94; Mat(t)hew, 36, 94; Philip, 32; Thomas, 62
Buckenham, New, places: beck (stream), 9, 13, 15, 17, 36, 65, 75; Bishop's Haugh/ Haugh Field, 12-15, 65-8, 70; Boulter Hill, 19; Brands Hill, 37; Chapel Street, 60; church, 19, *and see* grave slabs; common *see* commons; Dovehouse Yard, 36; gameplace, 15; gildhall, 15, 17, 49, 66; inns *see* inns, named; King Street, 36-7, 47, 60, 68; market cross/tolhouse, 15-19, 43, 57; market place *see* market; Marsh Lane, 38; mill, 13, 50-1; moat *see* moats; 'pinchpot hawll', 45; Priory manor in, 14; Spittlecroft, 68; Tan Vat Meadow, 36; *see also separate index of Reconstruction properties (p. 111)*
Buckenham, New, subjects: assets, 74; attractions of, 64; borough charters, 14, 74; borough organisation, 10, 14; charter box, 39; courts *see* courts; fair *see* fair; high bailiffs *see* bailiffs, high; history, 9, 14-16; housing stock, 10, 43-4, 64; law suits, 10, 15, 50, 73; minister, 14, 58, 71; St Martin's gild, 66; trading links, 34, 75
Buckenham, Old: 29, 34, 39, 45, 52, 54, 57-60, 62, 66-9, 78; Brokeshold, 62; castle and park, 9, 13, 35, 45, 58, 65, 72; Coole/High Field, 12-13, 65-6, 68-9, 73; Harling Wood, 13, 29, 62; poor, 73; priory, 28, 69
Bunwell, 69, 73, 78
Burgate (S), 34
Burgh (S), 57
Burrell: Stephen, 41, 49; William, 41
Burroughs, Samuel, 38, 47, 94
Burton: Henry, 63; William, 63
Bury St Edmunds (S), 36, 57
butchers and butchering, 16, 23, 26, 31, 35, 37-8, 51-4, 56, 61, 63-4, 70, 74-5, 77-9, 82
butchery/meat market, 15, 19, 26, 51, 54, 68, 74-5; regulation of, 25-6
Butterfeilde, John, 38
buttons, 33
Buxton, Francis, 27
Byrredge *see* Beredge

cabinet maker, 82
Cambridge university, 29, 65, 67, 71
candles, 33, 58, 86
Cann, Francis, 70
Carian (Carion): John, 36, 66, 94; Robert, 36, 66, 94
Carleton Forehoe, 29
Carleton Rode, 26, 29, 33-4, 45, 50, 54, 66, 69, 71, 73, 78; common, 13, 65, 67; windmill, 51
carpenters, 16, 62, 77, 80-2
carpets, 85
carrier, 82
Carter, ..., 62
Cary, Ralph, 50
Catlyn, Nevil, 54, 64, 94
cattle, 12, 52-3, 55, 60, 62, 68-9, 71
caupones *see* tapsters
Cawdwell, John, 72
chamber pots, 71, 88; urine from, 25
Chamberlain, Robert, 63
Chambers: Geoffrey, 52, 61, 94; William, 61
chandlers, 33, 56, 58, 78, 82
chapels *see* church *and* Dissent
chapmen/pedder, 16, 33, 78
charities, 14-15, 42, 47, 69, 73-4; records, 10, 16, 98; trustees' occupations, 10, 14, 79-80
Chase: family, 42; Margaret, 41; William, 41
cheese, 33
chimneys, 62; brick, 46; clay, 62; defective, 42, 46, 49-50, 61
church/chapel, building and repair, 61, 66; scales kept in, 19
churchwardens, 31n, 62, 71, 74
cistern, 49
Clarke: family, 33; Henry, 33, 50, 94; John, 33, 50; Peter, 19; Richard, 31, 58; Samuel, 33
clerks, 41, 83
clock, public, 15
clock reel, 27
cloth production and trade, 16, 26-34; finishing, 74; textile trades, 77-8; *see also* dyers, shearman, tenters
cloth, various, 30, 32-4, 84-5; *see also* weavers
clothier, 37
clothing, 62, 69, 84, 87

Cobbe, Robert, 56n, 94
collar maker *see* harness
Colman: John, 71; Thomas, 30-1, 71, 94; William, 62, 81
Colynder, William, 35, 38
commons and wastes, 10, 12-13, 36; hemp pits, 27; rights, 15; sheep excluded, 52
Compton census, 12
Constable, Whittney, 70
Cooper: John, 63, 94; William, 50, 94
coopers/hoopers, 63, 75, 77, 79, 83
Coote, William, 54
Copping, George, 53
cordwainers *see* shoemakers
counter table, 62
courts, borough, 10, 14, 20, 35, 67, 98; leet, 14, 41, 73; market, 14, 29, 55; portman, 14
Craske: John, 33; Peter, 26-7, 31; Robert, 26, 84
Cringleford, 26
Crowe: Charles, 58; family, 48; John, 46, 48-9, 58, 80, 94; Katherine, 46-7, 49, 58; Richard, 30, 80
Cubitt, Thomas, 26
curriers and currying, 16, 21, 35, 38, 47, 74, 77, 82
Curteis, Richard, 31, 82, 95
Cuson, Thomas, 29
cutler, 61, 77
Cuttler, Thomas, 61
Cuttyng, Thomas, 42, 73, 95

D'Albini: Earl William I, 9; family, 10, 14
Dade, Roger, 19
dairy and dairying, 55, 67, 69
dairy products, 19, 25, 33, 42, 50, 78
Davy, John, 54
Dawes, Anne, 29n, 95
Daynes: Nicholas, 36-7; Thomas, 55
Deb(b)enham, John, 57, 80, 95
deerskins, 35
Denny(e), Thomas, 32, 33n, 39n, 95
Dereham, East, 71
Desaguliers, John Theophilus, inventor, 59
Dey: family, 71; George, 66, 68-9; Isabel, 68; John, 54, 68; Robert, 55, 66, 68-9, 95
Dickerson, Francis, 25
Dickleburgh, 67, 78
Diss, 26, 30, 34, 38, 78; breweries, 46-7; market, 26

Dissent, 30, 32, 38, 75-6; meeting house, 76
doctors *see* medical men
dogs, 14; dogskins, 35, 38-9
dovehouse 35
Dowghty, John, 32, 45, 72-3
Downes, Thomas, 46, 95
drapers/woollendrapers/linendrapers, 16, 20, 28-35, 46, 49, 56-7, 60-1, 63-4, 67, 75-7, 79-82; drapery, 33
Dyer, Edward, 35
dyers and dyeing, 16, 27-8; dyehouse, 28; dyes, 33

earthenware, 58
East India Company, 69
Easton, John, 65
Eccles (by Attleborough), 34, 52, 78; Bishop's manor in, 12; parson, 14-15
Edmonton (Middlesex), 33
education, 38, 56, 59, 69; schoolmasters, 15, 41, 77, 83; schools, 32, 59n, 73; university, 29, 67
Edwards, John, 27, 48, 60, 95
eggs, 19
Eldred: family, 67; John, 66, 69, 95; Peter, 66, 69
Ellingham, Great, 39, 78
Elsden, John, 70
entertainment, public, 45, 59
esquire, 13, 65, 70, 79
excise officer, 82
Eye (S), 48
Eyton *see* Ayton

fair, 15, 17, 32
farming, farmers, 45, 54-5, 60, 63-71, 75, 82; implements, 62, 68
farms, development of, 70
Feeke, John, 70
Felstead, Humphrey, 61
feltmaker, 33
Fenn, John, 81
Fersfield, 78
fire, regulations/risk, 14, 36, 50, 60, 75
Fis(s)her (Fesher): Francis, 28, 95; James, 85, 88; Thomas, 71, 85, 88
fish: herring, 55; sprats, 55
fishmarket, 19, 35, 55; regulation of, 26
fishmongers, 55, 74, 77
fletcher, 63, 77

INDEX

forestalling, 25, 50, 55
forgery, 46
forges, 17, 24-5, 29, 60-1, 67, 75
Forncett, 55
Fortescue, Sir John, 46
Foulger: family, 39; Roger, 39
Fowler, John, 33
frankincense, 33, 87
Freemen, John, 46, 56, 95
Frier, William, 55
Fulcher: Sarah, 57n, 95; Thomas, 57, 80
fuller and fulling, 28
Fundenhall, 30
funeral arrangements, 53, 61
furnishings, 46, 48, 68, 85, 88-90; carpets, 52, 67, 85; looking-glass, 72; painted/stained cloths, 69, 89

Gage, ..., 27
Gall, John, 63
gamekeeper, 82
gameplace, 15
gaming, 42, 70
Garboldisham, 26, 78
garden house, 31
gardeners, 70, 77
gardens, 49, 69-70; physic, 56
geese, 14, 66
gentlemen/gentry, 13, 27-31, 38, 41-2, 45-9, 53-4, 57-9, 64-7, 71, 75, 79, 83
Geyton, Robert, 42
Gibbs: John, 49, 58, 82; Mary, 57, 82; William, 48-9, 56-8, 80, 95
Gibson, Thomas, 40
Gill, Robert, 42, 64n, 95
gingerbread maker, 26, 75, 77
Girling: Francis, 52-3, 95; Nicholas, 52, 95; Thomas, 52-3
Gissing, 39
glassware, 58, 71
glaziers, 54, 62-3, 77, 80-3
glovers, 35, 38-9, 74, 77, 80, 82
God(d)ard: John, 63, 81, 95; Mr, 82
gold and/or silver items, 29, 45, 67-9, 88
Golde, Thomas, 62, 95
Gooch: family, 30-2, 67, 76; Frances, 30, 95; John, 29-30, 38, 76, 95; Stephen, 29, 34, 47, 71, 76, 95; Thomas, 30
Gosse, William, 37, 54
Gostling, Charles, 15, 65, 70

grain (barley, corn, maslin, oats, rye), 19, 25, 29, 46, 50-1, 60, 68-9, 86; merchant, 78
grave slabs/tombstone, 30-1, 38n, 53, 54n, 57, 68, 71n
graziers, 23, 38, 51-4, 64
Green: Robert, 52; Thomas, 37
Grey, William, 27, 95
Grig(g)es: Lionel, 84; Stephen, 33
grocers and grocery, 16, 24, 26, 31, 42, 49, 52, 54-8, 66, 74-5, 77, 79-82; groceries, 33, 84-7
g(u)ildhall, 15, 17, 49, 66
Gye, Edward, 81

haberdasher, 32-4, 55-6, 66, 75, 77, 79, 83; haberdashery, 33, 84, 87-8
Hacon *see* Hagon
Hadman, John, 38, 95
Hadyson, Edward, 62
Hagon (Hacon), Edward, 32, 95
Hall, Richard, 51
Halyett, John, 49
Hapton, 26, 78
Hardingham, benefice of, 71
Harleston: 26, 28, 34; market, 26
Harling, East, 25, 29-30, 33-4, 57, 65, 78, 84-5; chalk from, 35; market, 26, 34
harness, 85, 90
harness/collar makers, 16, 40, 80, 82
Harnwell (Harmwell), William, 59, 64, 95
Harvey, Mr, 54
hats, 32-3
hatters, 32, 74, 77
Hawes, William, 72
hawkers, 25
Hawkynge, John, 84
Hayward, John, 39
Helmingham *alias* Morton, 69
hemp pits, 27
herbage, 14-15
Hickling, 65
Hingham, 78
HMS Princesse, 70
Hockham, 78
Hockley Hole, near London, 29
Holland: Bryant, 72; John, 54
Holyngshed (Cheshire), chapel, 66
Holynshed: Agnes, 66, 95; William, 66, 95
hoopers *see* coopers
hops, 41, 48; hop ground/poles, 48, 73

Hornigold, Henry, 55, 95
horsemill, 51
horses, 45, 51, 53, 68-9, 85; horse racing, 45, 59
hose *see* stockings
hosiers, 27, 81-2
house: building/repair, 61-2, 68, 70; rooms, 45-6, 52, 55-7, 62-3, 69
Howchin, Thomas, 37
Howell *alias* Howye, John, 61, 95
Howes *see* Huls(t)e
Hubbard (Hubbert): John, 32; Robert, 25, 84; William, 37
huckster *see* hawker
Huls(t)e *alias* Howes, Richard, 45-6, 61, 64, 95
Huntyng, John, 57, 60
husbandman, 12-13, 42, 45, 51, 55, 69
Hyde (Ide): Samuel, 50

immigrants, 14, 73
Ince, John, 32, 95
inns, named: Bell, 48; Black Bull, 45; Broadgate, 47; Bull Inn, 39, 42, 45, 50; Crown, 45-6, 49, 72; George Inn, 34, 40, 46-7, 49, 57, 69, 72; King's Arms, 48; King's Head, 47-8, 59; Lyon, 45-6; Rampant Horse, 48; Star, 48; Swan, 47, 57; Three Feathers, 30, 46; White Hart, 45-6, 56; White Horse, 48, 59
inns, taverns and innkeepers, 16-17, 22, 42, 45-50, 56-7, 59-60, 63-4, 66-7, 69, 72-5, 77, 79-80, 82; disorderly, 42, 45; *see also* tapsters
insurance, 49
ironmongery, 33, 87

Jackson's brewery, 141
Jacques, John, 38
Johnson: John Roome, 54; Mary, 55; Roger, 55
joiner, 62, 77, 80-2
Jolley, Thomas, 34
Josse *see* Killingworth
Juby (Joby): Dorothy, 47; family, 46, 69; John, 55; Robert, 69, 95; William, 45, 47, 49, 55, 66, 69, 95
Juce *see* Ince

Keddington family, 64

Kemp: Christopher, 48; Robert, 70, 95; Thomas, 48
Kendall *alias* Tendall (Tindall): Batylde, 55, 67, 97; family, 30, 41, 61, 64-5, 67-8; Henry, 29, 31, 42, 48-9, 51, 61, 66-8, 70, 97; John, 29, 48-9, 60, 66-8, 97; Katherine, 51, 68; Maurice, 57; Richard, 29; William, 29, 34, 60, 67, 97
Kenninghall: 26, 34, 68, 78; market, 26
Keteringe, William, 63
Kett, Richard, 26, 48
kiddier *see* hawker
Killingworth *alias* Josse, Robert, 51
kilns, 35, 49
Kimin, John, 47, 95
King's Lynn, market, 33
Kinge, Elizabeth, 32, 81
knacker *see* ropemaker
Knettishall (S), 69
Knyvett: Sir Edmund, 66; family, 10, 35, 54, 66, 75; John, 30; Mr, 69; Thomas, 45; Sir William, 66

labourers, 70, 82
lactage, 14
Lambard, William, 32
landgable, 10, 17-18
Lane, Samuel, 37
Langcroft, 67
Langdon, Clement, 71n
Langmere, 67
Larling, 30, 59
lawyers, 49, 57, 64, 68, 71, 75
leather goods, 35; production and working, 35-40, 74; regulation of, 35, 38; trade, 26
Lessingham, Richard, 76
limepits, 35
Lincoln(e): Henry, 50, 64, 95; Mr, 82; Thomas, 31
linen, 31; industry, 27; shop, 33; *see also* drapers, weavers
Lister, Isabel, 33n, 68, 96
Little Ouse valley, 34
Locke: Peter, 64, 96; William, 71n, 96
locksmith, 16, 60, 77
London, 56, 59, 69, 71; Fleet Prison 32; Gresham College, 59; Inns of Court, 67; *see also* Edmonton; Hockley Hole
Lopham, South, 30, 57
Lovell: Dionisia, 65n, 96; family, 65; John,

INDEX

65, 71
Lowestoft (S), church, 61
Lynford Hall, 68

maintenance agreements, 32, 56
malt, 19, 25, 34, 47, 51, 86
maltsters and malting, 26, 31, 42, 45, 48-9, 51, 54, 58, 64, 71, 74, 77-9; malthouses and mill, 22, 45, 47-9, 57-8, 74-5
Mane, Stephen, 39n, 96
maps and plans, 10
Marcon, John, 46, 49, 96
Marjoram (Margeries), Francis, 32
market and market place, 9, 15-19, 25-6, 33, 44-7, 50, 52, 54, 57, 60, 63, 67, 74-5; cross *see* Buckenham, New; decline, 16; reordering, 16-17; stallage, 12; stalling gear, 71; stallingers, 53
market days, regional pattern, 26
marriage gown, 69
marshes (marrishes), 12-13, 15, 17, 33, 36, 38, 43, 65-6, 68-9
masons/bricklayer, 62, 77, 82
Mat(t)hew, John, 39, 96
maypole, 33
meadows, 15, 36, 52-4, 58, 62, 68-70
medical drugs and instruments, 56-8
medicine/medical men, 42, 56-9, 74; *see also* phlebotomist, physicians *and* surgeons
Meene (Meine, Minns, Mynn): Anthony, 59, 96; family, 54; Henry, 31, 45, 49, 96; Robert, 26-8, 96
Megson, Robert, 60
mercers, 26, 28-9, 31, 64, 75, 77, 79, 82
merchants, 29, 48, 52, 59, 66, 69
merchant-tailor, 32, 81-2
metal workers, 75
Miles (Myles): Agnes, 46, 52; family, 27-8; John, 28, 32, 96; Robert, 28; William, 28, 96
militiamen, 33
Miller (Myller): John, 50; Robert, 25, 50; William, 50
miller, 51, 77
milliner, 16, 32, 74, 81-2
mills *see* windmills
Minn(s) *see* Meene
minstrel, 69
moats, 67; town moat/ditch, 15, 17, 31, 36, 70, 72, 75
Money, John, 76

Moore *alias* Mower: family, 54; William, 37
Morley, Richard, 71, 96
Morten (Murton, Moulton): Edmund, 38; Robert, 50; Rose, 50, 96; Simon, 50; William, 66
Morton *see* Helmingham
Moulton, 78
Moulton family *see* Morten
Mountague, Richard, 41
Mower *see* Moore
Muddiclift: Hannah, 58; James, 58; Thomas, 58, 96
Mundes, John, 60
Munnings, William, 36
Murton *see* Morten
Musculus, Wolfgang, *Commonplaces*, 33
musical instruments, 71-2
Mynn *see* Meene

Ne(a)ve (Newe): John, 68, 96; Thomas, 66, 68, 70, 96; Walter, 36, 68, 96; William, 36, 66
Netherlands, 33; *see also* Rotterdam
Norman: Henry, 32; Isaac, 38; Jane, 32; Robert, 27, 96
Norris, Robert, 48
Norwich stuff, 84
Norwich, 26, 32, 34, 48, 65-6, 69-70, 85, 88; bishop of, 9, 12; parish of St Augustine, 42; sphere of influence, 75; textile trade, 28
Nunn: Charles, 30-1; Henry, 39, 96; John, 39; Robert, 38-9

oatmeal, 42; oatmeal makers/making/sellers, 49, 51, 74, 77-9; oatmill, 19, 22, 51
occupations *see under individual trades*
orchards, 12, 14-15, 37, 49, 65-6, 68, 70
Orford, John, 39, 96
Osnabruch, Germany, 92
Ostler, William, 39
Ouse, Little, Valley, 34

Page, James, 55
painter, 27, 72, 77
Palgrave (S), 34, 57
Palmer, Clement, 39, 96
papists *see* recusants
Paris, France, Blue Nuns, 59
Parish (Parrys): Elizabeth, 72; Robert, 72; Thomas, 72

patten maker, 82
Payne (Pain): family, 60, 76; Hannah, 37n, 38, 96; John, 29, 32; Stephen, 38, 60-1, 66, 96
Pearson (Pereson): Richard, 30n, 37-38, 48n, 96; William, 37
pedder *see* chapman
Peke, Davye, 84
Perkins, Francis, 72
perukemakers, 47, 72, 80, 83
Perye (Perry), Richard, 70, 96
pewter, 85, 88-9
phlebotomist, 72
physicians, 24, 56, 58, 64, 75, 77
pightle, 70
pigs, 12, 25-6, 52, 60
pinner, 33
pipemaker, 72, 77
Pitcher, John, 71
plasterwork, decorative, 42
plumber, 63, 81-2
Plume, John, 36, 96
pointmaker, 33
Poll, John, 72, 96
poor, 10-11; apprentices, 27, 32, 39, 51, 70; attitudes to and relief, 42, 73-4; records, 10, 98; settlement bond, 39
poorhouse/workhouse, 46, 48, 83
population, 10, 12, 76
pot shop, 58
Pottle(s) (Pottell): Elizabeth, 42; family, 42, 60; Isaac, 42, 45, 49, 96; Joseph, 42, 45, 50, 60, 81, 96; Simon, 42, 45, 60, 96
poultry, 60; market, 19
preaching charity, 69
Prethero: Mr, 82; Owen, 37-8; Thomas, 37, 96
publican *see* inns
Pyknett, John, 32

Quidenham, chalk from, 35

rat poison, 33
Rattlesden (S), 37
Read, Charles, 39
Reconstructions, the, 10n, 15n, 16, 18, 63, 98-9
recusants (papists), 50, 59, 68
reeders, 16
Reynolds, (Reinoldes): Alice, 45; John, 27;
Simon, 45, 72, 96
Richards: family, 54; Francis, 81; Mary, 81; Thomas, 37, 54, 80-1, 96
Richardson, Nicholas, 32
Risbye, ..., 62
Rishangles (S), 34, 70
Robinson, Austen, 62
Rockland, 78
Rolfe, John, 51
ropemaker (knacker), 27
Rose: Hannah, 37; Joan, 37n, 96; John, 37; Robert, 37, 50, 80
Rotterdam, Netherlands, 72
Rowett (Rowed, Rowhede): Ann(e), 53, 56; Elizabeth, 56; family, 31, 54; Thomas, 56, 96; William, 56, 96
Roydon (by Diss), 67, 78
Rudland, Edward, 27
rum, 58
Rush, Thomas, 39, 96
Rushford, 64
Rushmer, John, 27, 81
Russell, Richard, 34, 96
Rysing, Robert, 35, 38

saddler, 36, 77
Salmon, John, 81
salters, 19
sandhole, 35
Sandy, Thomas, 80
sawyer, 62, 77
Saxham, Great (S), 69
Scarfe, Henry, 45, 96
Scarning, 59
schools *and* schoolmasters *see* education
Scots, campaign against, 31
scrivener, 71, 77
Segoe, Jane, 48
Semecroft, William, 67n, 68, 96
servants, 53, 60, 83
Shales: John, 52; Robert, 52; William, 51, 61, 96
Shardelowe: Doll, 71; Nancy, 71; Thomas, 71, 96
Sharpyng, John, 39
shearman, 20, 28, 32, 46, 52, 63, 78; equipment, 28
sheep, 52-4
Shelfanger, 39, 78
Sherman: John, 31; William, 31, 96

INDEX

Shickle, William, 48
Shoemaker, Hugh, 16
shoemakers and cordwainers, 16, 19, 35, 37-9, 61, 63, 74-7, 79, 82
shoes and boots, 35, 38
shop, illicit, 61
shopkeeper, 18, 82
Shortis, Stephen, 81
Shropham, 78
silkman, 28, 31, 75
silver *see* gold
Smith (Smyth): family, 32; John, 27, 32, 63; Thomas, 63, 96; William, 71
smiths *see* blacksmiths *and* whitesmith
Snare: Anne, 72; Clement, 72, 97; Thomas, 72
soap, 33, 84, 86-7
Spede, Robert, 56, 97
Spencer, Henry, 45
spices, 33, 85, 87
spinners/spinsters, 27
Spurgeon, John, 84
stable, 27
Stacey (Stacye): Osbo(u)rne, 29n, 42, 97; Stephen, 27, 50, 72, 97
Stagg, William, 53, 54n, 97
Stanton (S), 34
Steele, Edward, antiquary, 53
Stepney, Richard, 32, 81
steward, 30, 71
stockings/hose, 27, 29, 33
stocks, 15
Stone, Robert, 27, 97
Stradbroke (S), 69
Sturdevant (Sturdivant), Richard, 28n, 64, 97
Sturgeon, James, 49, 97
Styward, William, 66
Sudbury, Christopher, 48
sugar candy, 33
surgeons, 24, 47-8, 57-9, 75, 77, 80, 83
Swangey Fen, 9
Sword, William, 62
swords, 33

tailors, 16, 20, 29, 32, 77, 79, 82
Talbot, John, 65, 97
tanners and tanning, 16, 21, 36-7, 53-4, 56, 63-5, 68, 75, 77-82; equipment for, 36; regulation of, 35; tanneries, 35-8, 65, 72, 75

tapsters (*caupones*), 31, 33, 41-2, 48, 50, 52, 69; regulation of, 41
taxation and tolls, relief from, 15, 74
Taylor (Tayllor): Daniel, 51, 97; Godfrey, 51; Peter, 16
Tendall *see* Kendall
tenters, 20, 28
Thet, River, 9
Thetford, 51, 78; market, 26; mayor, 68; priory, 56
Thetford, Roger, 85, 88
Thorne, Thomas, 80
Thorney, Leonard, 33, 97
Thwayte, John, 61, 81
Tibenham, 34, 52, 66, 68-70; rectory, 65
timber, 19, 29, 52, 61-2; merchant, 52, 62
timber framing, 61
tithe, 14
Tivetshall, 34, 78
tobacco, sale of, 32, 45, 58, 72-3, 75, 77; pipes, 72, 75; suit (law) concerning, 27, 32, 39, 72-3
Tollis, John, 62
tolls, 19, 51; *see also* taxation
Tompson, John, 40
toothpicks, 71
trade token, 40, 56
Tunmore, Thomas, 46, 49
Turner, Robert, 33-4, 55-6, 66; inventory, 84-93
turnips, 51; cart, 62

Underwood: Peter, 42; Robert, 62; Thomas, 61, 97
Utting, Richard, 62

Verby: Robert, 60, 97; William, 60
Verdon: Agnes, 66; family, 64, 68, 71; John, 15n, 66, 73, 97; Jonas, 67, 74, 97; Robert, 66n, 97; William, 55, 64, 66-7, 73, 97
Vincent, Robert, 71, 85, 97
vintners, 41, 43, 47, 77

Wade: family, 49; John, 48-9, 80; Robert, 30-1; Thomas, 57, 97; William, 30-1, 34, 36, 58, 66, 80, 97
Walpole: Horatio, 49; John, 34, 49, 57-8, 80, 97; Mary, 57n, 97
Walsham, North, 68
Warden, family, 27, 30; John, 28; Robert,

28, 64n, 97
warehouses, 57-8
Warne: Edward, 30-1, 58, 97; family, 46; Rebecca, 30
Warner, Henry, 56, 97
warren, 45; warreners, 10
watchmaker, 72, 82
Watt(e)s: Francis, 40, 56; George, 56, 97
Watton, 78; market 26
Waveney valley, 34
Waynforth, Richard, 48
Wealden house, 32, 44, 61, 63
weavers, 27, 29, 34, 69, 77, 82; darnick, 26-7, 31, 49, 74, 79; linen, 27, 34, 48, 77, 80, 83; worstead, 26-7, 30-1, 63, 77, 80, 82
Webster, Robert, 39, 97
Welham, Elizabeth, 63n, 97
Well(e)s, William, 84
wells, 27, 36, 52, 55, 69
Wharton, Thomas, 47
wheelman, 82
whipping post, 15
whitesmith, 83
Wickes, Robert, 55n, 72n, 97
wigs, 72, 75
Wilby, 34, 39, 78; warren, 45
Willett, John, 58, 97
windmills, 13, 42, 50-1, 68, 74
windows: oriel, 46; painted glass, 40, 47
Winfarthing, 30, 39, 59, 68, 78
Witherell, Henry, 71
Wolward (Woodward): Henry, 47, 97; Lore, 48
Womac, Mr, 82
women, occupations of, 10-11, 16, 27, 32, 41, 46-50, 55, 81
Woods: Josiah, 39, 97; Josias, 39, 97; Obediah, 39, 97; Thomas, 61; William, 39
Woodward *see* Wolward
woodworkers, 61-3, 75; tools, 62
Woodyard, George, 33n, 97
wool, 33
woolcombers, 27, 30, 32
woollen cloth *see* cloth, drapers, weavers
workhouse *see* poor
Wren: Charles, 65; Christopher, 65
Wright: Charles, 51; Gregory, 51, 97; John, 49, 51
Wymondham: 26, 32, 34, 41, 78; brick/tiles from, 62; Congregation, 76; market, 26

Yallop, Nicholas, 49, 71, 97
Yarmouth, Great, recorder of, 68
yellow ochre, 85
yeomen, 12-13, 28-9, 33, 36-9, 42, 45-6, 48, 50-1, 54-6, 60-1, 63-4, 66-70, 75, 79
Youngman: John, 52, 60; Stephen, 42

Index of Reconstruction properties (*see* Fig. 4)

R1	27, 52-3, 62-3
R2	60-1, 65, 67-8
R3	36
R4	15, 31, 36, 52, 55, 60, 65, 70
R5	15, 31, 36, 52, 65, 70
R9	33
R10	38, 61-2
R11	38, 58, 60
R12	35, 43, 48, 57-8
R13	27, 57, 63
R14	26
R15	38, 62-3
R16	36, 39, 50-1, 66
R17	37
R18	36-7, 72
R19	39, 44
R20	44, 52, 62
R21	61
R22	26
R23	47, 52, 57
R24	26, 35-8, 54
R25	44, 56, 59-60, 70-2
R26	61-2
R27	63
R28	39, 40, 63
R29	32, 40, 63
R30	52, 61, 63
R31	27, 32, 39, 57, 61, 70
R32	60
R33	27, 52, 54n
R34	50, 67
R35	19, 50
R36	50, 67
R38	52, 61, 67
R39	32, 52, 68-9
R40	27, 29, 32, 63
R41	27, 30, 61, 64
R43	27, 49, 58
R44	48-9
R45	56
R46	19, 51
R47	42
R48e	39
R48f	29, 54
R49	32, 39, 44, 61, 63, 72
R50	32, 58-9
R51	45-6, 69
R52	45, 50, 56, 62, 72
R53	28, 32, 39
R54	29, 60
R55	29-30, 46, 49, 60
R56	38, 47, 52, 54, 59, 63, 67
R57	31, 36, 57, 84
R58	31, 36, 57
R59	31, 39
R60	28, 39, 61, 63
R61	63
R62	38-9, 57
R63	50, 63
R64	36, 39
R66	27, 48, 54, 59, 61, 67
R67	27, 48, 54, 59, 61, 67
R68	67
R69	32, 43, 54, 67
R70	50, 62
R71	50, 62
R72	52, 62
R73	42, 52, 60
R74	34, 40, 42, 46, 57
R75	27, 33, 58, 63, 72
R76	39
R77-9	33, 50
R80	40, 44, 52, 56, 60, 62, 72
R81	16, 32, 44, 53-4, 58, 63
R82	52, 54
R83	16, 28, 30, 46, 52, 69
R84	28, 30, 53, 57
R85	53-4, 56, 69, 72
R86	31, 36, 50, 53, 86
R87	50

You may also like

Norfolk and Suffolk Churches

The Domesday Record

David Butcher

available from local bookshops and www.poppyland.co.uk